CHECKMATE NARCISSIST

METHODS OF COUNTER MANIPULATION AND EMOTIONAL AIKIDO

LIUBOV GULBRANDSEN

DISCLOSURE

This book is designed to provide information that the author believes to be accurate regarding the subject matter discussed. No warranty is made concerning the accuracy or completeness of the information contained herein. Both the author and the publisher specifically disclaim any responsibility for any liability, loss, or risk, personal or otherwise, that may result directly or indirectly from the use and application of any of the contents of this book.

Furthermore, this book is not intended to serve as the basis for any personal decision. It should not be interpreted as a recommendation for specific actions, or advice. Each case is individual. Readers are encouraged to seek professional guidance tailored to their unique situations.

The author incorporates examples of real stories from real people; however, many names and identifying characteristics have been changed to protect their privacy. The narratives included are illustrative and should not be construed as endorsements or guarantees of any particular outcome.

By reading this book, you acknowledge and accept that the information provided is for informational purposes only and that you assume full responsibility for any actions taken based on the content herein.

CONTENTS

PREFACE

In the quiet corners of a seemingly perfect relationship, the sinister threads of manipulation can often go unnoticed until the weave is too tight, trapping you in a bewildering maze designed by a narcissist. In these moments, when the subtle signs morph into a clear pattern of emotional abuse, you might feel the most isolated and powerless.

Narcissistic abuse is not confined to one area of life - it can permeate your work, disrupt your romantic life, and strain familial bonds. Acknowledging this dynamic underscores the vital nature of this book. The need for these insights is widespread, touching countless lives just like yours.

I remember a friend of mine who was on the brink of losing her sense of self because she was overwhelmed by her partner's manipulative tactics. The transformation she underwent through learning and applying the strategies discussed in this book was profound. Stories like hers drive my commitment to this work.

I've crafted this book because I am deeply committed to supporting individuals like you - those who find themselves up against the daunting cunning of narcissistic personalities. Whether you're navigating the choppy waters of a romantic relationship, the deceptive calm of professional interactions, or the complex dynamics within your family, the insights and strategies here are designed to offer you clarity and control.

The core aim of "Checkmate Narcissist" is to arm you with the knowledge and tools necessary to recognize your vulnerabilities, apply emotionally intelligent tactics, and ultimately neutralize the narcissist's influence in your life. Through each chapter, we will journey from understanding the nuanced psychology of narcissism to applying effective counter-manipulation techniques. You will learn not just to cope but to thrive.

At the heart of our exploration is emotional intelligence - a powerful tool not only for defending against narcissistic maneuvers but also for building a resilient sense of self. By enhancing your emotional intelligence, you fortify your boundaries and cultivate a deep, inner resilience.

INTRODUCTION

In my previous book "Sleeping With a Narcissist", I described the most basic types of manipulative tactics used by narcissists. We talked thoroughly about gaslighting, blowing hot and cold, neglect, blame-shifting, triangulation, projection, isolation.

We also explored cycles of abuse and the role of hormones, such as Oxytocin, Dopamine, and Cortisol, in building co-dependency in our relationships with a narcissist.

In this book we will address the most frequently asked question - how to outsmart a narcissist.

Outsmarting a narcissist while playing by their rules is impossible. However, breaking their game and setting your own rules is possible.

The most important and the most challenging aspect of this game is managing your own emotions. More accurately, it's not about managing them but about tracking and understanding them. Manipulators play on our feelings, fears, instincts, and traumas.

I am not saying that we can independently rid ourselves of our traumas, which would require years of work with a psychotherapist. Undoubtedly, working through our traumas with a specialist would be very beneficial, although we would not be protected from new traumas.

The only thing that can protect us from further traumas and unpleasant scenarios with manipulators is our ability to recognize our emotions.

In emotional states, we often do not act as we intend. We get "stuck" or "carried away." I want to do one thing, but my emotions put me in a stupor or negatively affect my thoughts.

However, we cannot simply switch from one state to another. Confidence and insecurity come from within. Thorough processing takes time. We can learn to act appropriately and reasonably because self-management is a developable skill.

We can learn to make better decisions. We can learn to manage our emotions, and make it difficult for our opponent to unbalance us. This gives us the opportunity to act based on reality rather than on what our opponent tries to impose on us. This helps us move towards where we want to go rather than where we are being led.

Let's consider three main types of states in which you might find yourself when, for example, your partner starts yelling at you.

State One – Confusion

You freeze when your partner starts behaving aggressively or shouting at you. You're thinking, "Oh my God! What did I do wrong?" You're in shock, silent, sifting through options in your head. Then, you nervously mumble, "Is something wrong?" We will refer to this state as **self-doubt**.

State Two – Indignation

At this moment, you're thinking: "Okay! What is this idiot unhappy about? He's going to nitpick about something again! I'll leave, and then he'll see how bad it is without me!" If you go down this path, you might blurt out something seemingly harmless like, "What's going on?!" But your voice and facial expression betray your feelings - they are filled with resentment. We will categorize this attitude as **overconfidence.**

State Three – Interest

You are relaxed and a bit surprised. You're thinking, "Wow, what an upset look he has! Maybe something serious happened that he's struggling with. Can I help with something? I need to be careful with him right now." Then you speak with warmth and slight concern in your voice: "Is everything okay? Do you want me to come back later?" This may seem strange right now, but we will define this interest as **self-confidence**.

In all the three scenarios we felt and acted differently. The effect will also be different. In which of the three scenarios did we want to know what was happening because we felt the person's emotions, and in which did we feel concerned about how their dissatisfaction would affect us? Where did we empathize with our partner, and where did we worry about our fate? Where was our interest focused on ourselves, and where was it on the other person? If you remain in a calm, you are coming from the perspective that everything is fine with you. However, if you become tense and want to clarify the situation to protect yourself

- you observe uncertainty and overconfidence at work. The objective is to start seeing that we create these states within ourselves and that circumstances do not lead us into them.

In a state of self-doubt, we question whether everything is alright with us. The most frightening scenarios rush through our imagination, and our minds begin to frantically search for a way out - what will happen next? We feel bad, we are scared, we are tense. Our primary goal at this moment is to adapt. Our bodies and my brains are operating in survival mode.

In a state of overconfidence, we still doubt whether everything is alright with us. However, unlike self-doubt, we try to prove to ourselves and others that we are strong. In the second case, just like the first, we do not feel solid ground beneath our feet. To reduce anxiety and not feel weak, we turn on "confidence" and choose to think that "he is the fool." This gives us a pleasant feeling of superiority, and we begin to behave provocatively.

To find ourselves in a state of self-confidence, we need to remember and feel that everything is alright with us. We have a good attitude towards ourselves, and we trust ourselves and our intuition. We KNOW that everything is FINE. We control ourselves and, consequently, the entire situation. In this state we respond adequately. We do not succumb to the intimidation and provocations of our partner. Only in this state we can break their game scenario and lead the game by our own rules while also considering our interests.

CHAPTER 1
NARCISSISTIC SPECTRUM: FROM MILD TO MALIGNANT

I n my previous book, "Sleeping with a Narcissist," we covered the definition, traits and diagnostic criteria of narcissistic personality disorder. Today, millions find themselves entangled in emotionally disorientated, manipulative, and deeply damaging love relationships with narcissists.

In this book, we consider a wider spectrum of narcissistic influence on our lives, ranging from our family members and partners to colleagues and managers. I would like to revise some of the most essential characteristics and common manipulative tactics in narcissists' tool box. Understanding their methods of manipulations is an essential step before we proceed to counter-manipulation techniques.

1.1 KNOW WHO YOU ARE DEALING WITH

When you first meet a narcissist, the charm is palpable - the kind that sweeps you off your feet, fills the room with energy, and promises an electrifying connection. Narcissists do know how to make a good impression on you. They are magnetic and often misleading. This initial allure, however, can quickly unravel as the deeper, more manipulative traits surface, revealing a complex personality that poses a unique challenge in personal and professional relationships. This chapter aims to dissect the nature of narcissism, providing a robust framework to recognize and understand not just the overt displays of confidence, which might be essential for individuals to succeed in their businesses, but also the subtle signs of deep-seated insecurity and manipulation that characterize this condition. By delving into the clinical criteria, differentiating between various subtypes, and exploring how these traits play out across different areas of life, you will gain a comprehensive understanding of what you're dealing with and why it matters in your interactions with a narcissist.

Narcissistic personality disorder (NPD), as outlined in the Diagnostic and Statistical Manual of Mental Disorders, Fifth Edition (DSM-5), is defined by a pattern of grandiosity, a constant need for admiration, and a lack of empathy. These core characteristics form the basis of the disorder, but their manifestations can be nuanced and varied. For instance, grandiosity can appear as a superior attitude or an exaggerated sense of talent and achievement, often accompanied by fantasies about success, power, brilliance, beauty, or ideal love. The need for admiration is evident in the narcissist's excessive demand for praise and attention. A profound lack of empathy, a hallmark of NPD, is displayed through an inability to recognize or identify with the feelings and needs of others, which severely impairs interpersonal relationships.

Distinguishing between overt and covert narcissism is crucial for understanding the different manifestations of its traits. Overt narcissists are the ones you might think of first: they are outwardly self-confident, assertive, and often aggressively push to get their way. They revel in their status and achievements and are visibly hungry for admiration. Covert narcissists, on the other hand, might not immediately stand out. They tend to be quieter, harboring feelings of inadequacy and displaying hypersensitivity to how others perceive them while also feeling entitled to special treatment. Both types manipulate emotionally to meet their needs, but the methods and expressions differ significantly.

The continuum of narcissistic traits suggests that these character-istics can range from normal personality variations to extreme, pathological forms. It is crucial to understand that not everyone displaying confidence or concern about their image fits the criteria for narcissistic personality disorder. Narcissism becomes pathological when these traits are inflexible, maladaptive, and persisting, causing significant functional impairment or subjective distress according to the DSM-5 criteria.

Understanding how these traits affect relationships is essential. In personal relationships, the narcissist's partner often feels under-valued, ignored, and undeserving, as the narcissist fails to recog-nize their emotional needs. In professional settings, a narcissist can either be a charismatic leader who brings success but at the cost of creating a toxic work environment or a covert underminer who breeds unease and discontent. The challenges and conflicts in dealing with narcissists arise largely because of their lack of empathy, their entitlement, and their deep need for excessive admiration, which can lead to exploitative and abusive behaviors.

To further enhance your understanding, take a moment to reflect on past interactions with individuals who may have exhibited narcissistic traits. Think about how these interactions made you feel and write down any patterns you noticed. This exercise aims to help you identify and articulate your experiences, which is a critical step in learning how to effectively deal with narcissists in your life.

Understanding narcissism requires a nuanced appreciation of its spectrum, where behavior ranges from traits that are often considered normative to those that are intensely destructive and disruptive. This spectrum is pivotal to recognizing that narcissistic characteristics can be present in many people to varying degrees and do not always constitute a disorder unless they lead to significant impairment or distress. At the milder end, individuals may display what can be considered personality quirks - occasional selfishness, an expectation of special treatment, or a desire for admiration. These traits might manifest in everyday situations, such as a colleague frequently steering conversations to highlight his or her achievements or a friend who seems overly concerned with his or her image on social media. Though potentially irritating, these traits do not usually disrupt the individual's overall functioning or relationships in a significant way.

However, as we move along the spectrum towards malignant narcissism, the characteristics intensify and become more damaging. Malignant narcissists exhibit behaviors that are not only persistent and pervasive but also severely exploitative, manipulative, and deceitful. They often engage in aggressive manipulation tactics without remorse, exploiting others to achieve their own goals. This might include sabotaging colleagues to ascend in their careers or manipulating a partner's emotions to maintain control in a relationship. The lack of empathy, which is a common thread across the spectrum, becomes stark here, coupled with a readiness to harm others to serve their self-interests. The effects on those around them are often profound, leading to significant emotional and sometimes physical distress.

Consider the case of John, a senior executive known for his charismatic leadership and visionary ideas. Initially, his team was inspired by his confidence and ambitious goals. However, over time, it became evident that John had little regard for the well-being of his colleagues. He would set unrealistic expectations and publicly criticize those who questioned his authority, creating a climate of fear and anxiety. When a major project failed due to his risky decision-making, instead of taking responsibility, John manipulated the narrative to blame his team, leading to several unjust dismissals. This example underscores the destructive effects of malignant narcissism in a professional setting, where the drive for personal success results in collateral damage to others.

The spectrum of narcissism helps us understand that these traits do not exist in isolation; rather, they can be viewed on a continuum influenced by various factors, including upbringing, personal experiences, and possibly genetic predispositions. Recognizing where individuals might fall on this spectrum is crucial in determining how to interact with them effectively and protect oneself from potential harm. For those dealing with narcissists, especially at the malignant end, it becomes essential to adopt strategies that prioritize personal safety and emotional well-being, which might require professional intervention or the support of mental health experts.

In summary, the narcissistic spectrum serves as a framework for understanding the varied manifestations of narcissistic traits from mild to severe. By recognizing these patterns, individuals can better navigate their relationships and professional interactions and, when necessary, seek appropriate support or intervention. This spectrum also highlights the importance of context in assessing behavior, as traits that are problematic in one setting may not necessarily be so in another. Understanding this can help manage expectations and interactions more effectively, providing a basis for healthier relationships and personal boundaries.

1.2 THE NARCISSIST'S TOOLBOX: COMMON MANIPULATIVE TACTICS

Narcissists are often likened to skilled magicians, their manipulative tactics being the sleight of hand that distracts, distorts and ultimately deceives. These tactics are not used at random; rather, they are part of a calculated strategy to maintain control and dominance. Among these, gaslighting, triangulation, and projection stand out as particularly insidious techniques that can destabilize and disempower their targets, leading to significant psychological distress. Understanding these tactics in detail not only demystifies the actions of a narcissist but also empowers you to recognize and counteract them effectively.

Gaslighting, a term derived from the 1944 film "Gaslight," where a husband manipulates his wife to the point where she doubts her sanity, is a common technique used by narcissists to undermine the victim's perception of reality. By denying or distorting information, the narcissists cause their victims to question their memory, perception, and even their sanity. For instance, if confronted about a lie, a narcissist might flatly deny having said something, even if there is clear evidence to the contrary, insisting that the victim is remembering it wrong or is too sensitive. This tactic can lead to significant confusion and self-doubt in the victim, eroding their ability to trust their judgment and perceptions.

Triangulation involves the use of third parties to validate the narcissist's perspectives and invalidate those of the victim. By bringing another person into the dynamics of the relationship, the narcissist creates an alliance that helps isolate the victim and reinforce the narcissist's viewpoint. This can occur in any relationship and often involves the narcissist speaking negatively about the victim to others or talking directly to the victim about others to sow discord and create an environment where the narcissist appears in control and justified in his of her behavior. The psychological effect here is significant, as the victim feels alone, unsupported, and misunderstood, which can lead to isolation and depression.

Projection is another tool in the narcissist's arsenal, where the narcissist accuses the victim of embodying their negative traits or intentions, effectively deflecting blame and keeping the victim on the defensive. For example, deceitful narcissists may accuse their partners of lying, creating a scenario where the victims are too busy defending themselves to challenge the narcissists' behaviors. This behavior not only protects the narcissist from accountability but also adds a layer of confusion and conflict to the relationship, further destabilizing the victim.

To counter these tactics, it is crucial to establish a strong sense of self-confidence and rely on verified facts. Documenting interactions, maintaining a support network that provides validation, and setting clear boundaries are basic but effective strategies that can help protect against these manipulative techniques. Recognizing the tactic at play is the first step; the next is consistently reinforcing your boundaries and seeking external support to maintain perspective and sanity in an environment that seeks to distort both. Awareness and preparedness are your best defenses in navigating and countering the manipulative tactics of a narcissist, setting the stage for deeper exploration and more sophisticated strategies in the chapters to come.

The effects of narcissism on a victim's self-esteem and psychological well-being cannot be overstated. Continuous exposure to narcissistic behavior can lead to serious mental health issues, including depression, anxiety, and complex PTSD. Victims often report feelings of worthlessness, a loss of identity, and an overwhelming sense of betrayal. Recognizing this pattern is crucial for victims to start to detach their self-worth from the narcissist's manipulations, gradually regaining their independence and self-esteem.

Survivor stories offer powerful testimonies to the devastating effects of this cycle and the potential for recovery. Consider the experience of a woman who entered therapy after a tumultuous relationship with a narcissistic partner. Initially, she struggled with severe depression and self-doubt, unable to understand how the loving partner she once knew could turn so hurtful and indifferent. Through therapy, she learned to recognize the phases of the narcissistic cycle, which helped her make sense of her experiences and validate her feelings. Her journey to recovery involved reconnecting with her own needs and values, slowly rebuilding her life free from the narcissist's shadow. These stories are not just narratives of pain but of resilience and hope, underscoring the possibility of healing and renewal from post-narcissistic abuse.

1.3 NARCISSISTS AT WORK AND HOME: RECOGNIZING DIVERSE CONTEXTS

The influence of a narcissist seeps into every crevice of life, manifesting uniquely in professional environments compared to personal relationships. At work, narcissists often rise to positions of power, leveraging their charisma and strategic manipulation to outshine colleagues and sway superiors. Their tactics might include taking undue credit for collaborative projects, undermining peers to spotlight their contributions or manipulating team dynamics to ensure they remain the focal point of leadership's attention. For example, consider a scenario where a narcissist is part of a team project. They might initially contribute enthusiastically, positioning themselves as indispensable. However, as the project progresses, they may begin to shift responsibilities onto others, set unrealistic deadlines, or withhold crucial information, setting colleagues up to fail while they emerge unscathed and seemingly more competent.

In personal and home environments, the tactics of narcissists are more insidiously woven into the fabric of intimate interactions. Here, their manipulation often revolves around emotional control and dependency. Tactics might include gaslighting a partner about past events, isolating them from friends and family to increase dependence, or fluctuating between emotional warmth and coldness to create a state of confusion and attachment. This dynamic is painfully evident in romantic partnerships, where the narcissists' partners often find themselves making excuses for the narcissists' behaviors, trapped in a cycle that alternates between brief moments of romantic love and prolonged periods of deep emotional pain.

Navigating these treacherous waters requires tailored approaches that adapt to the nuances of each context. In the workplace, it's crucial to maintain professional boundaries and document interactions that can later substantiate any claims of unfair treatment. Regularly updating supervisors or HR departments about one's contributions and challenges can also counteract a narcissist's narrative. For instance, keeping email records and meeting minutes can provide a factual basis that counters any attempts by the narcissist to distort reality. Additionally, cultivating a diverse network of allies within the workplace can provide a bulwark of support and validation that mitigates the isolating tactics employed by narcissistic individuals.

In personal relationships, setting boundaries is equally crucial but often harder to enforce due to the emotional and sometimes physical closeness. It's essential to have clear lines about what behavior is acceptable and what isn't. Engaging in therapy, both individually and as a couple (if the partner is willing and sincere about change), can offer valuable tools and insights. Support groups and counseling can provide the emotional backing needed to make difficult decisions, such as ending the relationship if the narcissistic behavior becomes abusive or intolerable.

Legal and ethical considerations also play a significant role, especially in professional scenarios where narcissistic abuse intersects with harassment or discriminatory practices. Understanding one's rights within the workplace and the legal recourses available is essential. Many regions have laws protecting employees from emotional and psychological abuse at work, and knowing these can empower individuals to take decisive action when necessary. Consulting with legal professionals who specialize in employment law can provide guidance tailored to the specific circumstances, ensuring that actions taken are both justified and effective. Ethically, it's vital to handle such situations with professionalism, maintaining one's integrity even in the face of provocation and ensuring that any claims made against the narcissist are substantiated and documented to avoid potential backlash.

In every interaction with a narcissist, whether at work or home, the key is to remain informed and prepared. Understanding the specific manifestations of narcissistic behavior in these differing contexts allows for strategic planning and response, which is crucial in mitigating the effects of their actions. It empowers individuals to maintain control over their professional and personal lives, making informed decisions that prioritize their well-being and professional advancement. Knowledge and preparedness disempower the narcissist, stripping away the chaos and confusion they sow to maintain control. By fostering environments where transparency, respect, and integrity are prioritized, individuals can effectively diminish the influence of narcissistic behaviors and foster healthier, more productive interactions in all areas of life.

1.4 GENDER AND NARCISSISM: UNDERSTANDING DIFFERENCES IN BEHAVIOR

The landscape of narcissism, as intricate and varied as it may be, reveals distinctive patterns when viewed through the lens of gender. Research indicates that narcissism often manifests differently in men and women, influenced by both biological predispositions and socio-cultural conditioning. Men are statistically more likely to exhibit narcissistic traits and be diagnosed with narcissistic personality disorder than women. The higher prevalence in men is traditionally linked to cultural norms that encourage men to be assertive, self-assured, and competitive - qualities that can overlap with narcissistic traits, such as authority and self-sufficiency.

In contrast, female narcissists may exhibit their traits in less overt, more covert forms. They might manipulate through victimhood or martyrdom, leveraging societal expectations of women to be nurturing and submissive. These behaviors can often go unrecognized as narcissistic, as they superficially align with the caretaking roles women are frequently encouraged to adopt. Women with narcissistic tendencies might also focus more on exploiting interpersonal relationships than overt displays of grandiosity, making their manipulation subtler and possibly more insidious.

The cultural context significantly shapes how these behaviors are perceived and addressed. In societies with rigid gender roles, symptoms of narcissism in men might be celebrated as leadership qualities, whereas in women, the same behaviors could be criticized as overly aggressive or domineering. This disparity affects not only the recognition and diagnosis of narcissism but also the support systems available to victims. Men may receive accolades for their assertive behaviors, overshadowing the underlying exploitative tendencies, while women may be admonished, with their behaviors being framed as emotional instability or hysteria.

The gendered lens also profoundly affects relationship dynamics with narcissists. Men who exhibit narcissistic traits might dominate their relationships, expecting subservience and admiration from their partners, often leading to a dynamic where their partners feel overshadowed and undervalued. On the other hand, women displaying narcissistic traits might manipulate through co-dependency, creating relationships where their partners feel emotionally responsible and perpetually compelled to 'rescue' or 'fix' them. These dynamics are further complicated by societal expectations that men should not express vulnerability, which can prevent male victims of female narcissists from seeking help or even recognizing the abuse.

Addressing these complex gendered manifestations of narcissism requires tailored support systems that acknowledge and adapt to these differences. For men, support groups that focus on recognizing signs of emotional abuse and understanding narcissistic manipulation in all its forms can be invaluable. These groups can provide a safe space for men to express vulnerabilities without fear of judgment, challenging the cultural stigma around male victimhood. For women, literature and resources that highlight the specific tactics of female narcissists can be crucial in both recognizing narcissistic behaviors in themselves and identifying manipulation in relationships with other women.

As we continue to navigate and understand the multifaceted nature of narcissism, it becomes increasingly clear that gender plays a pivotal role in both the manifestation of narcissistic traits and the dynamics of relationships formed with narcissists.

CHAPTER 2
ROLES WE PLAY: CONDITIONING & SCRIPTS

The Role Theory explains that individuals have specific roles they play in different situations and contexts. People play these roles as members of a social group, family, or working group, which come with norms and expectations that dictate how individuals should behave. Over time, individuals can become accustomed to these roles, leading to automatic behaviors.

Behaviors and our reactions become automatic through repetition. When someone consistently plays a specific role in a situation, it can become a habit and initiate a so-called **"learned reaction"** to a particular trigger. In many situations, we react against our will or our interest just because we've "learned to react" this way. For example, when our partner starts yelling at us or a manager gives us a "silent treatment," it's a trigger for us that makes us react and behave in a certain way to avoid a conflict rather than stand our grounds.

In behavioral psychology, "Conditioning" (both classical and operant) refers to the ways in which behaviors can be learned and reinforced through repeated exposure to specific stimuli or situations.

Conditioning is a fundamental concept in behavioral psychology that explains how behaviors are learned and modified through interactions with the environment. Two primary types of conditioning are classical conditioning and operant conditioning. Each type involves different mechanisms and processes through which learning occurs.

2.1 CLASSICAL CONDITIONING & OPERANT CONDITIONING

Classical Conditioning

Classical conditioning, also known as Pavlovian conditioning, is a learning process that occurs through associations between an environmental stimulus and a naturally occurring stimulus. Ivan Pavlov, a Russian physiologist, first described this fundamental concept in behavioral psychology in the early 20th century. His research primarily focused on the relationship between stimuli and responses, using dogs as his subjects.

Pavlov was initially studying the digestive systems of dogs, specifically how they salivate in response to food. During his research, he noticed that the dogs would begin to salivate not only when food was presented but also when they saw the lab assistant who fed them or even when they heard the footsteps leading to their feeding. This observation led him to investigate the mechanisms behind this learned response.

Pavlov used a series of controlled experiments with dogs. He would isolate the dogs and measure their salivary response to food. When the dogs saw or smelled the food, it naturally triggered a salivary response. Pavlov then introduced a neutral stimulus, such as the sound of a bell. He would ring the bell just before presenting the food to the dogs. Initially, the ring of a bell did not elicit any salivation from the dogs.

Pavlov would repeatedly pair the neutral stimulus (bell) with the unconditioned stimulus (food). Over time, after several pairings, the dogs began to associate the sound of the bell with the presentation of food.

The bell became a "conditioned stimulus." The dogs would now begin to salivate in response to the bell alone, even when no food was presented. This response is known as the "conditioned response."

The four key components of this theory include conditioned and unconditioned stimulus, and conditioned and unconditioned response.

- *Unconditioned stimulus* is a stimulus that naturally and automatically triggers a response without prior learning (e.g., food).
- *Unconditioned response* is our natural, unlearned response to the unconditioned stimulus (e.g., salivation in response to food).
- *Conditioned stimulus* is a previously neutral stimulus that, after being paired with the unconditioned stimulus, begins to trigger a conditioned response (e.g., a bell sound).
- *Conditioned response* is the learned response to the conditioned stimulus that occurs after the association is made (e.g., salivation in response to the bell).

Pavlov concluded that the dogs had learned to associate the bell with food. This was an indication of classical conditioning, where a neutral stimulus becomes associated with an unconditioned stimulus to elicit a conditioned response. Thus, Pavlov demonstrated that learning occurs through the association of stimuli.

Classical conditioning can explain various phenomena, such as phobias, taste aversions, and emotional responses. For example, a person who has a negative experience with a particular food may develop a taste aversion to it if he/she becomes nauseated after eating it.

Operant Conditioning

Operant conditioning, introduced by B.F. Skinner, is a learning process in which behaviors are modified by their consequences, including rewards and punishments. This type of conditioning emphasizes the role of reinforcement and punishment in shaping behavior.

The key components of this theory include:

- *Reinforcement* - any consequence that increases the likelihood of a behavior being repeated. Reinforcement can be positive (adding a pleasant stimulus) or negative (removing an unpleasant stimulus), for example, giving a child a treat for completing homework, giving an employee a reward for a completed task, or giving a hug to your partner and saying nice words to him/her.
- *Punishment* - any consequence that decreases the likelihood of a behavior being repeated. Punishment can involve adding an unpleasant stimulus or removing a pleasant stimulus. Examples are taking away a toy when a child misbehaves, reducing or eliminating a bonus,

giving silent treatment in love relationships, or one
partner yelling over the other.

- *Shaping* - the process of gradually reinforcing behaviors
  that are closer to the desired behavior, effectively guiding
  us toward the desired outcome. This process teaches us
  to associate our behavior with the outcome, shaping our
  future behavior.

Operant conditioning is widely used in various settings, such as
education (rewarding good behavior), animal training (reinforcing
desired behaviors), and behavior modification programs (using
consequences to change maladaptive behaviors).

Both classical and operant conditioning are essential mechanisms
of learning in behavioral psychology. They illustrate how behaviors can be acquired, maintained, or modified based on experiences and interactions with the environment. Understanding
these concepts provides valuable insights into human behavior,
learning processes, and the development of habits.

2.2 HOW TO OVERRIDE YOUR CONDITIONAL REACTIONS

Overcoming conditioned behaviors and implementing new
habits and reactions involves a systematic approach that
combines self-awareness, intentional practice, and reinforcement
strategies. Outlined below are steps you can take to effectively
change conditioned behaviors and develop new habits:

Self-Awareness and Identification

- Recognize conditioned behaviors: Start by identifying the specific behaviors or reactions you want to change. Reflect on situations where you tend to react automatically due to conditioning.
- Understand triggers: Identify the cues or stimuli that trigger these conditioned responses. This could include emotional triggers, environmental factors, or social situations.

Set Clear Goals

- Set clear objectives for each encounter with a narcissist. Make sure your goals are specific, measurable, achievable, relevant, and time-bound (SMART).
- Define new habits: Clearly articulate the new behaviors or habits you want to adopt. Always keep your objectives in your mind.
- Visualize success: Imagine yourself successfully implementing these new habits and the positive outcomes that will result.

Create an Action Plan

- Start small: Begin with small, manageable changes to avoid feeling overwhelmed. Gradually increase the complexity or frequency as you build confidence.
- Use triggers: Identify positive triggers (cues) that can prompt the new behavior. For example, if you want to adopt a habit of exercising, set a specific time and place for your workouts.

Practice Mindfulness

- Stay present: Engage in mindfulness practices to enhance your awareness of thoughts and feelings. This can help you recognize when you are about to engage in conditioned behavior.
- Pause and reflect: Before reacting, take a moment to pause and consider your response. This can help you break the automatic cycle of conditioned responses.

Reinforcement Strategies

- Positive reinforcement: Reward yourself for successfully adopting new behaviors. This could be through small treats, self-praise, or other forms of recognition.
- Negative reinforcement: Remove an unpleasant stimulus when you successfully implement the new behavior (e.g., if you're trying to reduce stress, you might allow yourself to skip a chore for the day after completing a workout).

Use Habit Stacking

Link new habits to existing ones: Pair the new behavior with an already-established habit. For example, if you want to meditate, do it right after brushing your teeth each morning.

Practice Regularly

- Consistency is key: To override conditioned behaviors, practice the new behavior consistently. Repetition helps reinforce the new neural pathways associated with the desired behavior.

- Track progress: Keep a journal or use a habit-tracking app to monitor your progress. This can provide motivation and accountability.

Seek Support

- Accountability partners: Share your goals with friends, family, or support groups. Having someone to encourage you can be motivating.
- Professional help: Consider working with a therapist or coach who can provide guidance and support in changing conditioned behaviors and forming new habits.

Reflect and Adjust

- Evaluate: Periodically assess your progress. Reflect on what is working, what isn't, and why.
- Be flexible: If certain strategies aren't effective, be open to adjusting your approach. Experiment with different techniques to find what resonates with you.

Be Patient and Persistent

- Understand conditioning takes time: Remember that changing conditioned behaviors can be challenging and may take time. Be patient with yourself.
- Embrace setbacks: Understand that setbacks are a natural part of the learning process. Use them as opportunities to learn and grow rather than as reasons to give up.

By following these steps, you can effectively work to override your conditioned behaviors and reactions and implement new, positive habits and reactions in your life. The key is to remain committed, practice consistently, and be kind to yourself throughout the process.

2.3 SCRIPTS VS CONDITIONAL BEHAVIOR

In cognitive psychology, scripts are cognitive structures that guide behavior in specific contexts and help individuals understand and navigate specific situations based on past experiences. They represent the sequence of expected actions or events in a given situation and can lead to habitual responses.

Scripts serve as frameworks for predicting and interpreting events, guiding behavior in a structured manner, they help us **anticipate what comes next**.

Understanding Scripts

A script is a cognitive structure that outlines the typical sequence of actions or events expected in a particular context. It serves as a mental guide that helps individuals know what to expect and how to behave in specific situations.

The four components of scripts are:

- Scripts include typical actions or events, so called *prototypical events*, that occur in a particular scenario. Scripts allow individuals to process information quickly and efficiently, reducing the cognitive load in familiar situations. They guide how to behave, what to expect, and how to interact with others in a given context. Scripts help individuals predict the behavior of others, which can facilitate social interactions. We understand what to expect. For example, a restaurant script might include entering a restaurant, being seated, ordering food, eating, and paying the bill. When we go to a doctor, we arrive, check-in, wait, see the doctor, and check out. When we go Shopping, we enter a store, browse items, select products, check out, and leave.

- Scripts often have a chronological order, indicating the expected sequence of events, referred to as *temporal order*. It helps individuals anticipate what comes next. Scripts represent structured sequences of actions or events. They are more comprehensive and context-specific, focusing on the expected flow of events in familiar situations.
- Scripts often involve different roles (e.g., customer and waiter in a restaurant) and specify their interactions. Thus, they define *roles and participants*.
- Scripts are activated by specific *contextual cues* - in specific contexts or situations when the relevant cues are present - helping individuals recognize when to apply them. They guide behavior through a series of expected actions. They typically involve multiple actions and interactions, capturing a broader understanding of a scenario.

On the other hand, conditional behavior refers to responses that are triggered by specific conditions or stimuli, often involving a learned association between a stimulus and a response. This concept is often tied to learning through classical or operant conditioning, where behaviors are learned based on the consequences of actions.

The behavior is developed through reinforcement or punishment, where certain behaviors are encouraged or discouraged based on their consequences.

Thus, individuals might develop anxiety (behavior) as a conditioned response to hearing wedding bells (stimulus) due to a prior negative experience at a wedding or returning home where their partner is meeting them with silent treatment, or anger. Still, the consequence becomes evident to these individuals and causes anxiety even before they find out what happened or what their partner is dissatisfied with.

Conditional behavior is a **learned response** triggered by specific stimuli. However, by understanding the way it works and developing emotional intelligence, we can override our reactions, build new habits (scripts) and thus affect the outcome.

CHAPTER 3
BUILDING YOUR EMOTIONAL INTELLIGENCE

Imagine you're sitting across from someone who knows exactly which buttons to push to escalate a situation. Each remark and each gesture is calculated to draw a specific emotional response from you. In the realm of dealing with a narcissist, where manipulation weaves through interactions like a dark thread, the mastery of your own emotions isn't just helpful - it's crucial. This chapter delves into the foundations of emotional intelligence (EI), a set of skills that not only enhances your interactions with others but also fortifies your defenses against those who may seek to exploit your emotions.

3.1 FOUNDATIONS OF EMOTIONAL INTELLIGENCE: AN OVERVIEW

Emotional intelligence, popularized by psychologist Daniel Goleman in the 1990s, is the ability to recognize, understand, manage, and reason with emotions. It is a multifaceted skill set that encompasses self-awareness, self-regulation, motivation, empathy, and social skills. Each component plays a pivotal role in how we navigate our emotional landscape and interact with others. Self-awareness involves recognizing your own emotions and their effects; self-regulation relates to managing or redirecting disruptive emotions and impulses; motivation refers to harnessing emotions to pursue goals; empathy is understanding the emotional makeup of other people; and social skills involve managing relationships to move people in desired directions.

In conflicts, particularly those involving manipulative individuals like narcissists, EI can be your greatest ally. By leveraging these skills, you can maintain control over both the situation and your emotional state, preventing the narcissist from destabilizing the interaction. For instance, in a heated exchange, an emotionally intelligent response would involve recognizing your emotional triggers (self-awareness), calming yourself (self-regulation), understanding the underlying emotions of the narcissist (empathy), and navigating the conversation to a less confrontational place (social skills).

Theorists like Goleman underscored the significance of EI not just as a soft skill but also as a powerful tool for enhancing leadership, resilience, and interpersonal dynamics. Research in this field has shown that individuals with high EI tend to be more successful in both personal and professional realms. They handle pressure better, create stronger relationships, and are generally more pleasant to be around. Unlike IQ, which is relatively static, EI can be developed over time, providing an invaluable growth path for anyone, especially those dealing with complex personalities in their lives.

Understanding the difference between EI and IQ (intellectual intelligence) is crucial. While IQ might predict academic and professional achievement, EI plays a critical role in determining how we manage behavior, navigate social complexities, and make personal decisions to achieve positive results. In relationships fraught with emotional manipulation, a high IQ can provide the knowledge needed for recognition, but it is EI that offers the wisdom for effective response. It is the difference between knowing that someone is manipulating you and being able to shut down that manipulation gracefully and effectively.

Reflective Exercise: Evaluating Your Emotional Intelligence

Take a moment to reflect on a recent conflict or challenging interaction - perhaps with a colleague, friend, or family member. Try to identify which aspects of EI you used effectively and which areas could use improvement. Did you recognize your emotional state at the time? Were you able to regulate your responses to avoid escalation? How well did you understand the emotions of the other person involved? Reflecting on these questions can provide valuable insights into your current EI skills and highlight areas for further development.

As we progress through this chapter, we'll explore these components in greater depth, providing you with practical strategies to enhance your emotional intelligence. By doing so, you'll not only improve your personal and professional relationships but also build a robust defense against the psychological warfare often waged by narcissists. With enhanced EI, you stand a better chance of maintaining your emotional equilibrium and integrity in the face of adversity.

3.2 SELF-AWARENESS: RECOGNIZING YOUR EMOTIONAL TRIGGERS

Self-awareness is like holding a mirror to your inner emotional landscape. It's about gaining a clear view of your feelings, reactions, and the triggers that set them off. In relationships with narcissists, where emotional manipulation is the norm, recognizing your triggers is a critical defense mechanism. Narcissists have a knack for pinpointing vulnerabilities and using them to their advantage. By identifying these sensitive spots, you can fortify your defenses, reducing the narcissist's ability to disrupt your emotional equilibrium.

Consider the common triggers that might resonate with you. These could be feelings of inadequacy sparked by criticism, fear of abandonment stirred by cold or dismissive behaviors, or anger triggered by feeling disrespected or ignored. Narcissists often exploit these emotional triggers to maintain control and power in the relationship. For instance, if they know you fear criticism, they might use derogatory comments to keep you anxious and off-balance. Understanding your triggers helps you anticipate and neutralize these tactics, maintaining your emotional stability and regaining control of interactions.

Journaling is an excellent method for tracking these emotional triggers. By keeping a daily log of your feelings and the circumstances that surround them, you begin to see patterns emerge. This practice aids not only in identifying triggers but also in constructively processing emotions, rather than letting them simmer unchecked. Start by jotting down instances when you felt particularly emotional and note what happened just before that feeling emerged. Over time, this record will reveal specific conditions or actions that trigger negative responses, equipping you with the knowledge to handle them more effectively in the future.

Managing Stress Through Your Body

To learn to manage yourself and your emotional reactions, it is crucial to develop the ability to observe yourself from within as well as from an outsider's perspective. When you find yourself facing a manipulator, try to detach and imagine viewing yourself from above. Then, take a deep dive into your feelings - what emotions are present? Fear, anger, confusion? Where in your body do you feel these emotions?

Let's practice this. As you read this book, ask yourself: "How am I feeling right now? Am I in a comfortable position? Am I relaxed? Am I breathing calmly and deeply? Does my body feel good?" Perhaps you instinctively adjusted your posture, relaxed your shoulders, and took a deep breath. That's great! However, when you shift your focus to your body, many people find it hard to concentrate on the reading. When they return to the text, they often forget about their body, as if they can only focus on one or the other. Now, try to continue reading while keeping some awareness of your body - monitoring it as you go. For most people, this kind of attention management is unfamiliar, but it is fundamental to self-management. This is a skill we need to cultivate to maintain confidence and recognize attempts at manipulation.

Imagine the improvements in your life when you can consistently achieve this. You will think more clearly and resist others' influences. You will understand how to influence your state and choose how to behave. You will tackle your tasks in a way that supports you rather than hinders you. You will learn to be a true friend to yourself. If you take a break from reading, challenge yourself to observe your body during everyday activities - how it feels and whether that state is serving you at the moment. You will also learn to manage your state during stressful situations. A manipulator may attempt to scare you, throwing you off balance emotionally to disconnect your conscious reactions and trigger the unconscious impulses they need.

When we talk about "stress," we refer to the body's mobilization for survival. This involves the physiological restructuring of the organism when it shifts into a mode of fighting against perceived life-threatening threats. When we perceive a situation as dangerous, the body initiates a self-preservation program, depriving some systems of energy while enhancing others. Blood may rush to the arms and legs, slowing the functioning of internal organs. The abdomen and back may tense up as if bracing for impact. Breathing changes from steady to rapid and shallow. The chemical composition of the blood alters, with hormones released that are necessary for prolonged resistance or a desperate surge. All the body's resources are directed toward confronting the challenge, while rational thinking is suppressed.

The inability to manage ourselves comes at a high cost. In both business and personal communication, it creates numerous problems. Under stress, our habitual behavior mechanisms take over, and we overlook everything else because our attention becomes limited.

In stressful situations, we may forget our original intentions. Our instincts drive us, altering our goals. We might intend to do one thing but end up doing another. We may want to remain silent but instead find ourselves justifying our actions. We may wish to reach an agreement, yet fear can cause us to abandon our positions and agree against our interests, resulting in a highly emotional reaction.

If we can recognize in the moment how we start pressuring ourselves and how this affects our mood, we can stop it simply by choosing to do so. No extra effort is needed; instead, we can focus on relaxation and relief.

When we lack the skill to observe ourselves, we operate on "autopilot." Our instincts, beliefs, and habits make choices for us, ultimately controlling our reactions. Automatons lead us only to where they have been programmed, not where we truly want to go. In a state of stress, we become easy targets for manipulation.

Mindfulness Practices to Enhance Self-Awareness

Integrating mindfulness into your daily routine can significantly enhance your self-awareness. Mindfulness involves staying present and fully engaged in the current moment without judgment. This practice helps you observe your thoughts and feelings without getting entangled in them, providing clarity and insight into your emotional triggers. Simple techniques like focused breathing or mindful meditation can be powerful tools. For example, when you find yourself triggered, take a moment to breathe deeply and focus solely on the sensation of the air moving in and out of your lungs. This brief pause can help disconnect the immediate emotional reaction from the trigger, allowing you to assess the situation more calmly and respond rather than react.

Seeking feedback from trusted individuals can also enrich your self-awareness. Sometimes, emotions or biases can cloud our perceptions, making it difficult to see things clearly. Friends, family members, or therapists who understand that your goal is to improve your emotional intelligence can offer invaluable insights into how you respond to certain triggers. They can provide observations about patterns you may not notice yourself and offer alternative strategies for managing your reactions. This feedback loop, when approached with openness and a willingness to learn, can significantly accelerate your self-awareness.

As you enhance your self-awareness through these practices, you not only become better equipped to manage your interactions with a narcissist but also improve your overall emotional health. Recognizing and understanding your triggers enables you to navigate not just the challenging waters of manipulative relationships but all areas of life with greater calm and resilience. By turning inward and understanding the landscape of your own emotions, you set the stage for more meaningful and balanced interactions with everyone around you.

Here are some techniques that can help you quickly regain control over yourself:

1. Deep breathing: Practice deep breathing to calm your mind and body.
2. Body awareness: Tune into your body and identify where you feel stress, and then proceed to progressive muscle relaxation.
3. External perspective: Look at yourself from the outside.
4. Set goals: Establish your objectives for the conversation or distance yourself by imagining a cute baby hat on your opponent.

This can help you gain perspective and maintain control over the situation.

3.3 SELF-MANAGEMENT: TECHNIQUES TO CONTROL EMOTIONAL REACTIONS

The ability to manage your emotions effectively is more than just a skill; it's a vital aspect of navigating life, particularly when interacting with narcissists. Given their propensity for emotional manipulation, having strategies in place to control your reactions can significantly affect the outcome of your interactions with them. One effective technique is the practice of pausing before reacting, which can be as simple as counting to ten or taking a series of deep breaths. This brief moment allows you to step back from your immediate emotional response, providing space to assess the situation more objectively and respond rather than react impulsively. For instance, when a narcissist attempts to provoke you with a critical comment, this pause can be the difference between a heated argument and a controlled response that keeps you in charge of the interaction.

Stepping away from a stressful situation to regain composure is another practical approach. This could mean physically removing yourself from the environment where the interaction took place, or it could be a mental withdrawal into a calm state of mind. Techniques such as visualizing a peaceful scene or focusing on a task that requires concentration can effectively distract you from the emotional turmoil and reset your mental state. For example, if a discussion with a narcissistic partner becomes too intense, excusing yourself to take a walk or engage in another form of physical activity can help dissipate the anger or frustration, allowing you to approach the situation later with a clearer mind.

Maintaining your long-term emotional health is crucial not only for personal happiness but also as a defense mechanism against ongoing emotional manipulation. Regular self-care routines play a significant role in supporting your emotional stability. Engaging in regular physical exercise, for instance, not only improves your physical health but also has profound benefits for your mood and mental well-being, thanks to the release of endorphins. Adequate sleep and a balanced diet are equally important; they ensure that your body and mind are at their best and most resilient, equipped to handle the challenges posed by a narcissist. Establishing and maintaining these healthy habits can create a strong foundation, enhancing your ability to manage stress and reduce vulnerability to emotional manipulation.

Cognitive restructuring, a technique derived from cognitive-behavioral therapy, involves identifying and challenging negative thinking patterns that can arise from interactions with a narcissist. These might include thoughts like "I'm not good enough" or "I can't do anything right," which the narcissist may instill in you to maintain control. By questioning the validity of these thoughts and replacing them with more balanced and constructive ones, you can shift your perspective and reduce the emotional power these thoughts may hold over you. For instance, instead of thinking, "My partner always criticizes me because I'm incompetent," you could reframe it to, "My partner uses criticism as a tool for control; his/her comments do not define my worth." This shift in thinking can diminish the effects of the narcissist's words and help maintain your self-esteem.

Setting clear emotional boundaries is another essential aspect of self-management. It involves clearly defining what is acceptable and what is not in how others treat you, communicating these boundaries assertively and adhering to them even when challenged. For those involved with a narcissist, boundaries are often disregarded or challenged; therefore, being consistent and firm in maintaining them is crucial. Suppose a narcissist repeatedly tries to belittle you in public. In that case, a clear boundary might be stating, "I am not willing to continue this conversation if you continue to speak to me disrespectfully," and then disengaging if the behavior continues. Not only does this protect your emotional well-being, but it also sends a clear message to the narcissist about what behavior you will and will not tolerate, potentially deterring future attempts at manipulation.

Through these strategies, you can create a robust framework for managing your emotional reactions, which is essential for anyone dealing with the complexities of a relationship with a narcissist. By maintaining control over your emotional responses, you empower yourself to interact more effectively and protect your mental health, ultimately shaping the dynamics of your relationships in more healthy and respectful ways.

3.4 SOCIAL AWARENESS: READING THE NARCISSIST'S CUES

Understanding social cues in any interaction is akin to reading a map before you embark on a journey. When dealing with a narcissist, where every gesture and word can be part of a larger strategy, decoding these cues becomes even more critical. Nonverbal communication, such as body language and facial expressions, often tells a more truthful story than words alone. For example, while narcissists might be verbally expressing admiration, their non-verbal cues, like a dismissive hand gesture or a smirk, can reveal disdain or contempt. These subtle signs are red flags, signaling underlying narcissistic intentions or hidden agendas. Paying close attention to inconsistencies between what narcissists say and their body language can provide you with real insight into their motives, helping you navigate the interaction more strategically.

Moreover, the context in which interactions occur plays a significant role in understanding and predicting manipulative behaviors. A narcissist at a public event, for instance, might play the charming host to garner admiration from others while in private settings, his/her manipulative and controlling behaviors come to the forefront. Being mindful of these situational changes in behavior can alert you to the narcissist's manipulative tactics, helping you prepare and respond appropriately. Observing how narcissists treat others in different contexts can also offer clues about their true nature and intentions. This awareness prevents you from being caught off guard and allows you to maintain control over your interactions with them.

Emotional contagion, the phenomenon where one person's emotions and related behaviors directly trigger similar emotions and behaviors in other people, is another crucial aspect of dealing with narcissists. Narcissists often exude negative emotions - rage, frustration, disdain - that can be incredibly infectious, dragging you into their emotional turmoil without your conscious consent. Shielding yourself from these negative emotions is essential to maintain your emotional health. Techniques such as mentally stepping back from the situation, maintaining a calm and composed demeanor, and engaging in positive self-talk can help create a buffer against the emotional onslaught. Being aware of this risk allows you to actively fortify your emotional boundaries, ensuring that the narcissist's mood does not dictate your emotional state.

Cultural sensitivity is equally important in interpreting behaviors correctly, as cultural backgrounds can significantly influence how emotions and intentions are expressed. What might be considered a straightforward or assertive communication style in one culture could be seen as rude or aggressive in another. When interacting with a narcissist from a different cultural background, it is important to consider these nuances to accurately interpret their actions and intentions. This understanding can prevent misinterpretations and provide you with a clearer picture of the narcissists' behaviors, helping you respond more effectively. Being culturally aware not only aids in navigating cross-cultural interactions but also enriches your perspective, allowing you to interact with a broader range of individuals more successfully.

In summary, developing social awareness by reading non-verbal cues, understanding contextual influences, guarding against emotional contagion, and being culturally sensitive are all essential skills in dealing with narcissists. These skills enable you to anticipate and neutralize manipulation, maintain your emotional stability, and ensure more positive outcomes in your interactions. As you continue to hone these abilities, you'll find yourself not only better equipped to deal with narcissists but also more adept at navigating all your social interactions with greater confidence and insight.

3.5 RELATIONSHIP MANAGEMENT: NAVIGATING INTERACTIONS STRATEGICALLY

In the intricate dance of managing relationships, especially those complicated by the presence of a narcissist, strategy is not just beneficial - it's necessary. Effective relationship management involves mindful planning before interactions, employing tactful conflict resolution techniques during conversations, and knowing how to influence outcomes positively without manipulation. Additionally, mastering ways to decompress after particularly challenging encounters is crucial for your well-being. Each of these components plays a vital role in building a resilient interaction strategy that preserves your emotional health while navigating the complexities of relationships dominated by narcissistic behavior.

Strategic interaction planning starts with setting clear objectives for each encounter with a narcissist. This proactive approach involves anticipating potential issues and deciding what you want to achieve from the interaction.

For instance, if you're preparing for a discussion about household responsibilities with a narcissistic partner, your goal might be to establish a fair division of tasks. By entering the conversation with this clear objective, you can steer the discussion towards constructive outcomes rather than getting sidetracked by the narcissist's attempts to dominate or derail the conversation. It's helpful to visualize the conversation beforehand, imagining how you will respond to potential provocations and rehearsing calm, assertive responses. This preparation not only boosts your confidence but also equips you with a mental script that can guide you through the interaction, helping you stay focused on your goals.

Conflict resolution techniques are indispensable when dealing with narcissists, whose default interaction mode often involves some level of conflict. One effective method is the use of 'I' statements—these allow you to express your feelings and needs without sounding accusatory, which can help in de-escalating potential confrontations. For example, instead of saying, "You never help around the house," you could say, "I feel overwhelmed when I have to manage household tasks by myself." This approach communicates your feelings clearly and invites cooperation rather than conflict. Focusing on solutions rather than problems is another key strategy. By directing the conversation towards potential solutions and asking for the narcissist's input, you can engage them in a constructive dialogue that focuses on outcomes rather than blame.

Influencing a narcissist's behavior and decisions positively requires a subtle blend of affirmation and assertiveness. Narcissists crave admiration and are more receptive to suggestions when they feel their self-esteem is being boosted. Therefore, acknowledging their strengths or past contributions before presenting your views can make them more amenable to your suggestions. For example, you might begin with, "I've always admired how you handle financial planning," before introducing a budget-related request or suggestion. This tactic not only makes the narcissist feel validated but also increases the likelihood of a positive response to your proposals.

Finally, decompression techniques are crucial after interacting with a narcissist. These encounters can be mentally and emotionally draining, making it essential to engage in activities that help you recover and regain your equilibrium. Engaging in a hobby, such as painting or gardening, can be incredibly therapeutic. These activities allow you to focus on something enjoyable and fulfilling, helping to dissipate any residual stress from the interaction. Alternatively, talking things over with a supportive friend can provide emotional relief and a fresh perspective on the situation. Sharing your experiences and feelings with someone who understands can validate your emotions and help you process the encounter more effectively.

By integrating these strategic elements into your interactions with narcissists, you equip yourself with a robust toolkit that not only helps you manage these complex relationships but also protects and preserves your emotional well-being. Each strategy, from planning and conflict resolution to influence and decompression, serves as a critical component in navigating the challenging waters of relationships with narcissists, empowering you to handle interactions with confidence and resilience.

3.6 EMPATHY AS DEFENSE: UNDERSTANDING WITHOUT ENABLING

Empathy, often confused with sympathy, is about stepping into someone else's shoes and understanding their feelings and perspectives without judgment. This nuanced skill becomes particularly vital when interacting with narcissists, who are often skilled in eliciting sympathy and support to their advantage.

Empathetic listening, therefore, is not about condoning or agreeing with their distorted perceptions but about understanding the emotions behind their behavior. This deep level of comprehension allows you to navigate interactions wisely, recognizing the narcissist's emotional landscape without being drawn into their manipulative tactics. For instance, if a narcissist expresses anger or frustration, understanding that these emotions might stem from their insecurities or fears can help you respond in a way that addresses the emotion rather than the surface-level accusation.

However, the line between empathy and enabling can be thin and often blurred. It's crucial, therefore, to distinguish clearly between the two. Empathy involves understanding another's feelings and needs while maintaining your psychological distance. Enabling, on the other hand, occurs when empathy crosses into the territory of supporting or excusing the narcissist's harmful behaviors, thereby perpetuating the destructive cycle. To prevent this, it's essential to apply empathy judiciously, ensuring it doesn't lead to compromising your values or ignoring unacceptable behavior. Guidelines here may include acknowledging the narcissist's feelings without agreeing with their actions or expressing understanding while also stating your disagreement or discomfort with their behavior.

Utilizing what might be termed 'protective empathy' can be an effective strategy for managing interactions with a narcissist. By anticipating the emotional needs and likely reactions of the narcissist, you can prepare yourself to respond in ways that avoid conflict and minimize harm. For example, knowing a narcissist's need for admiration, you might choose to acknowledge their achievements in a conversation before addressing more contentious issues. This approach not only helps in maintaining a peaceful interaction but also protects you from becoming embroiled in unnecessary disputes.

Setting boundaries with empathy is perhaps the most challenging yet crucial aspect of dealing with narcissists. It involves expressing your understanding and care in a way that does not compromise your emotional well-being. This could mean saying things like, "I see that this is important to you, and I understand it upsets you, but I need us to discuss this calmly," or "I understand you're feeling upset; however, I will not tolerate being spoken to in that way." This approach ensures that you are acknowledging their feelings, thus not invalidating their experience but also firmly establishing how you expect to be treated. It's a delicate balance that requires practice and, often, support from others, such as through role-playing with a therapist or a trusted friend to build your confidence in maintaining these boundaries effectively.

Empathy, when used wisely, can be a powerful tool in your inter- actions with a narcissist. It allows you to understand their behavior and emotional triggers without getting caught up in their manipulative tactics. By practicing empathetic listening, distinguishing it from enabling, using protective empathy, and setting boundaries with empathy, you equip yourself with a nuanced approach that respects both your emotional health and that of the narcissist without compromising your integrity or well-being.

In summary, this chapter has explored the critical role of emotional intelligence in dealing with narcissists, from under- standing your emotional triggers and managing your reactions to navigating complex social cues and handling interactions strategi- cally. The skills developed here are not just tools for handling difficult people; they enhance all areas of your life, leading to richer, more fulfilling relationships and a stronger, more resilient self.

As we move forward, the next chapter will build on these foundations, focusing on specific strategies for counter-manipulation that empower you to not just survive but thrive in the face of narcissistic tactics. This next step is about turning insight into action, ensuring you are fully equipped to stand your ground and protect your emotional space effectively.

CHAPTER 4
THE AIKIDO APPROACH TO CONFLICT RESOLUTION: HARMONIZING RELATIONSHIPS THROUGH MOVEMENT AND UNDERSTANDING

Aikido, a Japanese martial art developed by Morihei Ueshiba, emphasizes harmony, where we blend with our opponent's energy, redirecting it rather than confronting it head-on. Its principles can be effectively applied to conflict resolution in various contexts, including personal disputes, workplace conflicts, or broader social issues.

The essence of "emotional aikido" is that a person does not openly oppose his/her opponent but tries to navigate emotions in the right direction.

Confronting and counter-attacking narcissistic behavior requires a strategic approach grounded in psychological Aikido principles. By employing techniques that redirect, reflect, and assert, you can navigate conflicts while maintaining your integrity and emotional well-being.

Applying these aikido principles to conflict resolution in conflict situations with a narcissist will allow you to approach disputes with a mindset focused on collaboration, understanding, and peaceful outcomes. This approach not only helps resolve conflicts but also serves as a shield from narcissists' aggression and pressure, fostering a more harmonious environment.

Aikido principles empower you to stand up against narcissistic manipulation without falling into aggressive patterns or losing your sense of self.

Embracing these techniques requires patience and practice, but the rewards are invaluable.

4.1 PRINCIPLES OF AIKIDO APPLIED TO CONFLICT RESOLUTION

Blending and Harmony

Aikido teaches practitioners to blend with an opponent's energy rather than opposing it directly. In conflict resolution, this means understanding others' perspectives and emotions. By acknowledging their feelings and viewpoints, one can create a more collaborative environment for resolving disputes.

Redirection

Instead of escalating a conflict, aikido practitioners learn to redirect an opponent's energy. In conflict resolution, this translates to finding constructive ways to steer a conversation or situation away from confrontation and towards cooperation. It could involve reframing the discussion or introducing alternative solutions that satisfy both parties.

Centering and Calmness

Aikido emphasizes maintaining one's center and composure even in the face of aggression. In conflict situations, remaining calm can help de-escalate tensions. Practitioners can focus on their breath and body awareness to maintain a sense of equilibrium, allowing for clearer thinking and more effective communication.

Non-Resistance

Aikido teaches that resistance can lead to greater conflict. In conflict resolution, this principle suggests avoiding defensiveness and instead approaching discussions with openness and a willingness to listen. By not resisting the other party's arguments, one can create a space for dialogue and understanding.

Empathy and Understanding

Aikido encourages practitioners to develop a deep sense of empathy, recognizing the humanity of their opponents. This strategy is very disarming. In conflict resolution, this means actively listening and seeking to understand the underlying needs and concerns of the other party, which can lead to more compassionate and effective solutions.

Focus on Resolution, Not Victory

Aikido practitioners aim to achieve a peaceful resolution rather than defeating an opponent. In conflict resolution, the goal should be to find a win-win solution where both parties feel heard and satisfied, rather than one side "winning" at the expense of the other.

Use of Space and Movement

In aikido, practitioners learn to control space and movement. In conflict resolution, this can mean being aware of the physical and emotional space between individuals, finding ways to create a safe environment for discussion, and encouraging movement toward collaborative solutions rather than entrenched positions.

Mindfulness

Aikido practice involves being present and aware of one's surroundings and actions. In conflict resolution, mindfulness can improve one's ability to respond thoughtfully rather than react impulsively, leading to more productive discussions.

Maintaining one's center is at the core of Aikido. The ability to stay grounded and composed is essential not only in mastering martial arts but also in navigating the complexities of human interaction, especially during conflicts. This chapter delves into the importance of centering and offers practical techniques to cultivate calmness in the heat of dispute.

When I say "centering," I refer to the state of being physically and mentally stable. In Aikido, it is connected to the concept of "hara," or the lower abdomen, which is considered the center of gravity and energy in the body. When practitioners are centered, they can move fluidly and respond effectively to an opponent's actions.

In conflicts, emotions can cloud judgment and lead to reactive behaviors. When individuals are uncentered, they may respond with anger, defensiveness, or aggression, escalating the conflict further. Centering allows one to approach the situation from a place of clarity and calmness, facilitating more constructive communication and resolution.

In the next chapters, we review non-confrontational methods of counter-manipulation, such as pseudo-agreement, reframing, and withdrawal.

4.2 KEY METHODS FROM AIKIDO THAT CAN BE APPLIED IN CONFRONTATION WITH A NARCISSIST

While the principles of non-resistance in Aikido provide a valuable framework for navigating conflicts, confrontation may sometimes be necessary, especially when dealing with narcissistic individuals who may push boundaries and engage in manipulative behavior. You will have to address the manipulative behavior, such as gaslighting with a confrontation, if it persistently violates your boundaries or in other situations where your well-being or the well-being of others is at risk.

It is essential to maintain integrity and respect during confrontations. A counterattack is sometimes necessary to reclaim your power and assert your boundaries. A mindful counter-attack can serve as a powerful tool to deter narcissistic behavior while remaining grounded in your values.

We all know that narcissists can exhibit disrespectful, dismissive, or damaging behavior. Recognizing when confrontation is necessary is key to maintaining your boundaries and integrity. Counterattack does not mean aggression; rather, it involves addressing the behavior directly and asserting your needs without compromising your values.

In Aikido, one of the fundamental skills is the ability to redirect an opponent's energy rather than confront it head-on. This principle is equally applicable in love relationships, where conflicts can arise from differing perspectives, emotions, or needs. This chapter explores redirection techniques in the context of romantic relationships, providing detailed examples and practical strategies to transform potential confrontations into constructive dialogues.

Redirection involves acknowledging the energy or emotion presented by your partner and skillfully steering the conversation or situation toward a more positive and constructive outcome. Instead of resisting or escalating the conflict, redirection encourages a collaborative approach that honors both partners' feelings.

Psychological Aikido techniques can empower you to assert yourself effectively while minimizing the potential for escalation. This chapter will explore how to confront narcissistic behavior while employing counter-attacking strategies rooted in psychological Aikido principles. These strategies include redirect technique, mirror technique, assertive statement, boundary reinforcement, tactical retreat, strategic questioning, and emotional detachment.

Three additional techniques, script breaking, generalization, and concretization, deserve a more detailed approach and are described in the later chapters of the book.

The Redirect Technique

Instead of meeting aggression with aggression, redirect the conversation to focus on the behavior rather than the person.

If a narcissistic colleague makes a demeaning comment during a meeting, you might respond with, "I find it difficult to contribute when the conversation is framed that way. Can we focus on the ideas instead of personal critiques?" This technique preserves your dignity while pushing back against inappropriate behavior.

The Mirror Technique

Reflect the narcissist's behavior to them in a non-confrontational manner to help them see the effects of their actions without feeling attacked.

If your partner frequently interrupts you, you might say, "I noticed that when I start to speak, I often get cut off. It makes it hard for me to share my thoughts. Can we try to let each other finish before jumping in?" These statements mirror their behavior and invite them to reconsider their approach.

The Assertive Statement

Use "I" statements to express your feelings and needs without placing blame. This technique fosters personal ownership of your emotions while clarifying your boundaries.

Suppose a friend with narcissistic tendencies continually monopolizes conversations. You could say, "I feel overlooked when I can't share my experiences. I'd appreciate it if we could balance our discussions." This assertive statement focuses on your feelings rather than accusing them, which can reduce defensiveness.

The Boundary Reinforcement

Clearly define your limits and communicate the consequences of crossing them. This technique emphasizes your right to self-respect while holding the narcissist accountable.

If a narcissistic colleague consistently takes credit for your work, you might say, "I want to clarify that I contributed significantly to this project. If this continues, I will need to document our contributions more formally." This assertive claim reinforces your boundaries and alerts them to the implications of their actions.

The Tactical Retreat

Sometimes, stepping back from a heated situation can provide the space needed to regroup and return with a clearer perspective. This technique avoids escalation while allowing you to reclaim your emotional energy.

If a conversation with a narcissist becomes too heated, you can say, "I need a moment to collect my thoughts. Let's take a break and revisit this later." This response not only de-escalates the tension but gives you time to strategize your approach.

The Strategic Questioning

Use questions to encourage the narcissist to reflect on their behavior or to clarify their intentions. This technique can help shift the focus from confrontation to inquiry.

If a team member dismisses another's idea outright, you might ask, "What makes you believe that idea won't work? Can we explore its potential further?" This approach encourages dialogue and may prompt the narcissist to reconsider their stance without feeling personally attacked.

The Emotional Detachment

We have previously spoken about maintaining emotional distance during confrontations. This technique allows you to respond rationally instead of reacting emotionally, which is crucial when dealing with manipulative behavior.

If faced with a barrage of accusations from a narcissistic partner, practice emotional detachment by saying, "I hear your concerns, but I need to process this. Let's take a moment to discuss it calmly." This acknowledgment separates your emotional response from their behavior, allowing you to remain grounded.

Reframing the Narrative

Reframing the situation in a way that highlights your perspective can change the context of the conversation to shift the dynamic without confrontation.

If your partner insists that their needs are more important than yours, you could say, "I understand your needs are significant, but let's also consider how we can meet both of our needs. It's important for both of us to feel valued." This reframing encourages mutual consideration rather than a one-sided focus.

If your partner says, "You never listen to me," acknowledge their feelings and suggest a solution. You could respond, "I understand that it feels like I'm not listening. Let's set aside some time this week to talk without distractions. I want to make sure I'm hearing you." This redirection transforms a potentially confrontational statement into a constructive dialogue.

The Power of Silence

Use silence strategically to create discomfort for the narcissist. This technique can force them to confront their behavior or to reconsider their approach.

If a colleague makes a snide remark, instead of immediately responding, pause and maintain eye contact. The silence can prompt them to reflect on their words, often leading to an apology or a retraction.

Highlighting Consequences

Make it clear that their behavior has consequences. This technique holds the narcissist accountable without resorting to aggression.

If a narcissistic boss belittles you in front of others, you might say, "I find it difficult to work effectively in an environment where I feel disrespected. If this continues, I may need to discuss this with HR." This claim communicates the seriousness of their behavior without attacking them personally.

Using Humor as a Shield

Humor can disarm a narcissist and turn the tables on their negative behavior. This technique allows you to assert yourself while defusing tension.

If a narcissistic friend makes a cutting remark, you could respond with light-heartedness: "Wow, I didn't know we were doing stand-up comedy! I'll be sure to prepare my best jokes for next time." This declaration counters their negativity with humor, demonstrating that their words don't affect you as intended.

Establishing Your Own Narrative

State your perspectives and intentions openly to take control of the narrative. This technique helps re-establish your identity and authority in the situation.

If a narcissistic partner distorts an event to make themselves look better, you might say, "I'd like to clarify what happened from my point of view. It's important for me that we're both on the same page." This clarification positions you as an active participant in the conversation rather than a passive recipient.

Seeking Support

In some cases, it may be necessary to involve a third party or seek support from mutual friends, colleagues, or supervisors. This technique can provide additional validation and reinforce your position.

If a colleague consistently undermines you, you could approach a manager and say, "I'd like to discuss some interactions I've had with [Colleague]. I believe they may be affecting our team's dynamic, and I want to ensure we're all working effectively together." This response not only addresses the issue but also protects your interests within a larger context.

Confronting and counter-attacking narcissistic behavior requires a strategic approach grounded in psychological Aikido principles. Techniques that redirect, reflect, and assert can help you navigate conflicts while maintaining your integrity and emotional well-being.

These methods empower you to stand up against narcissistic manipulation without falling into aggressive patterns or losing your sense of self. Whether through fact-checking, reframing narratives, using humor, or establishing boundaries, you can effectively counteract narcissistic behavior while fostering a healthier dynamic in your relationships.

4.3 EXERCISES TO HELP YOU WORK YOUR "GROUNDS"

Breathing Exercise

Find a quiet space and sit comfortably. Close your eyes and take a deep breath through your nose, allowing your abdomen to expand. Hold for a moment, then exhale slowly through your mouth, feeling the tension leave your body. Repeat this process for several minutes, focusing solely on your breath.

Application: Whenever you sense conflict arising, take a moment to breathe deeply. This simple act can help you regain composure and approach the situation with a clearer mind.

Grounding Techniques

Stand with your feet shoulder-width apart. Feel the ground beneath you and visualize roots extending from your feet into the earth. Imagine drawing energy up from the ground with each breath. This exercise helps establish a sense of stability and connection.

Application: In moments of conflict, visualize yourself rooted to the ground. This mental image can provide a sense of stability, reminding you to remain composed amidst emotional turbulence.

Body Awareness

Practice a simple body scan. Start from your head and progressively move down to your toes, noticing any areas of tension. As you identify these areas, consciously relax them, letting go of any tightness.

Application: Regularly checking in with your body can help you recognize when you are becoming uncentered during a conflict. By tuning into physical sensations, you can intervene before emotions escalate.

Mindful Movement

Engage in slow, intentional movements, such as Tai Chi or basic Aikido footwork. Focus on the fluidity of your movements and the connection between your body and your breath.

Application: Practicing mindful movement can help you cultivate a sense of calm and presence. During conflicts, moving with intention - whether through body language or pacing - can convey calmness and confidence.

Visualization Techniques

Visualize a peaceful place where you feel safe and centered. It could be a serene landscape, a quiet room, or anywhere that brings you tranquility. Spend a few moments immersing yourself in this visualization.

Application: When faced with a conflict, recall this peaceful image to help ground yourself. This mental refuge can serve as a reminder to remain calm and centered.

Even with the best techniques, maintaining composure during a conflict can be challenging. Remember, when tensions rise, take a moment to pause before responding. This brief interlude can prevent reactive responses and allow for more thoughtful communication.

CHAPTER 5
ADVANCED EMOTIONAL
TACTICS

I n the quiet aftermath of stormy interactions with a narcissist, the need for a sanctuary of calm becomes evident. This need brings us to a crucial aspect of dealing with narcissistic behavior: emotional detachment. Although it may sound like a cold withdrawal, emotional detachment is a strategic, healthy way to interact with someone who drains your emotional reservoir. It is about maintaining your inner peace, keeping your feelings in check, and not allowing yourself to be swept away by the turbulent currents of a narcissist's chaos. This chapter aims to arm you with the techniques necessary to cultivate this form of detachment, turning what might feel like an emotional battleground into a place of serenity from which you can engage safely and effectively.

5.1 MASTERING EMOTIONAL DETACHMENT: PRACTICAL TECHNIQUES

Understanding Emotional Detachment

Emotional detachment is the process of stepping back - emotionally and mentally - from a situation to prevent getting overwhelmed by negative emotions. It's a form of self-preservation that allows you to interact with a narcissist without getting caught up in their manipulative games. Importantly, emotional detachment is not about cutting off all emotions or becoming indifferent; rather, it's about controlling your emotional responses to protect your mental health. This skill is particularly valuable in situations where narcissists use emotional upheaval as a weapon, aiming to destabilize and control.

Detachment Techniques

One effective technique for fostering emotional detachment is mindfulness meditation. This practice involves focusing on the present moment without judgment, which can help you recognize and release unnecessary emotional involvement in interactions. By regularly practicing mindfulness, you can develop a clearer, calmer state of mind that enhances your ability to remain detached in stressful situations.

Cognitive reframing is another powerful tool. This technique involves changing your perspective on a situation to alter its emotional effect. For instance, instead of viewing a narcissist's insult as a personal attack, you can reframe it as a reflection of their insecurities. This shift in perspective can help you remain emotionally detached as you recognize that the issue lies with the narcissist, not with you.

Setting emotional limits is also crucial. Determine in advance how much emotional energy you are willing to invest in interactions with the narcissist and stick to this limit. When you feel this boundary being pushed, give yourself permission to step back or disengage, which might mean ending a conversation or taking a break from the interaction to prevent emotional overload.

Role-Playing for Practice

To build confidence in your ability to detach emotionally, consider engaging in role-playing exercises. These can be done with a therapist or a trusted friend. Simulate interactions you might have with the narcissist, practicing your detachment techniques. Role-playing allows you to experiment with different responses in a safe environment, helping you prepare for real-life interactions. For instance, you might practice using non-reactive language or maintaining a calm demeanor in the face of provocation.

Evaluating Progress

It is helpful to assess your emotional state regularly after interacting with the narcissist to gauge your progress in mastering emotional detachment. Reflect on whether you were able to maintain your composure, keep your emotional boundaries intact, and disengage before becoming overwhelmed. Self-assessment tools, such as journals or emotional check-ins, can be useful for tracking these reflections. Over time, you should notice an increased ability to engage with the narcissist without feeling emotionally drained or upset.

Reflective Exercise: Tracking Emotional Detachment

Consider maintaining a journal where you document your interactions with the narcissist, noting your emotional state before, during, and after each encounter. Reflect on techniques that helped you maintain detachment and situations in which you might have struggled to keep your emotions in check. This ongoing reflection can provide insights into your progress and areas for further development.

By mastering emotional detachment, you equip yourself with a vital skill that not only preserves your emotional health but also empowers you to interact with a narcissist on your terms. This approach allows you to protect your inner peace, enabling you to respond to manipulative behaviors thoughtfully and strategically rather than reactively.

5.2 THE POWER OF POSITIVITY: SHIELDING AGAINST NEGATIVITY

In the face of a narcissist's often pervasive negativity, cultivating a fortress of positivity around yourself is essential for maintaining your mental and emotional health. Think of positivity not as a mere mood but as a strategic shield capable of deflecting the harmful effects of narcissistic behaviors. This shield is constructed through deliberate practices, such as gratitude, the nurturing of positive experiences, and the reinforcement of your self-esteem through affirmations. These practices empower you not only to withstand the challenges posed by narcissists but also to thrive despite them.

Gratitude, for instance, is a powerful practice that can transform your perspective. It shifts your focus from what is lacking or problematic to what is abundant and right in your life. Start by keeping a gratitude journal, where each day, you jot down three things for which you are thankful. These don't have to be grand; even appreciating a sunny day, a delicious meal, or a supportive conversation can significantly shift your mood and outlook. This habit gradually changes how you experience your daily life, making it harder for a narcissist's negativity to penetrate your improved mental state. Over time, this practice can lead to profound changes in your overall emotional health, enhancing your resilience and reducing susceptibility to external negativity.

Positive affirmations are another cornerstone in building your positivity shield. These are empowering statements that, when spoken repeatedly, reinforce your self-worth and counteract the demeaning or manipulative messages from a narcissist. For example, if you find yourself being criticized unjustly, affirmations like "I am competent and valued" or "Others' opinions do not define my worth" can be a balm to the sting of harsh words. To integrate affirmations into your life, start by writing a list of positive statements that resonate with you and your situation. Repeat these affirmations in the morning or during moments of doubt to fortify your self-esteem against external attacks.

Surrounding yourself with positivity extends beyond internal practices to include the environment around you and the company you keep. Strive to cultivate a circle of supportive friends who uplift and encourage you. Engage with media that reinforces positive messages and inspires you - be it books, music, or films. Likewise, create a personal space that reflects positivity. Including elements like soothing colors, inspirational quotes, or plants can bring a sense of life and growth. Each of these elements acts as a buffer against the negativity that a narcissist might bring into your life, reinforcing your emotional health and resilience.

Reflection Section: Building Your Positivity Shield

Reflect on the current state of your surroundings and relationships. Consider whether they reflect positivity and support or whether changes could enhance your emotional environment. Think about the media you consume and their effects on your mood and outlook. Are there books, music, or shows that could be replaced with more uplifting alternatives? Reflecting on these aspects of your life can help you make deliberate choices that enhance your positivity shield, making you more resilient in the face of negativity.

A positive outlook does more than just counterbalance the negative; it actively enhances your resilience, enabling you to bounce back from setbacks more quickly and with less distress. When you cultivate a habit of seeing the good, learning from experiences, and moving forward with optimism, you develop a kind of emotional buoyancy. This resilience is invaluable not only in dealing with narcissists but in all areas of life where challenges and setbacks are inevitable.

By embracing these practices and fostering a positive environment, you equip yourself with the tools to maintain your emotional equilibrium and thrive, regardless of the challenges you face. This proactive approach to cultivating positivity ensures that the negativity of others does not derail your sense of self or your emotional well-being, allowing you to live a more fulfilled and balanced life.

5.3 TRANSFORMING VULNERABILITY INTO STRENGTH

When interacting with a narcissist, your vulnerabilities might initially appear as weaknesses, easy targets for exploitation. However, recognizing and redefining these aspects of your psyche can transform them from points of fragility into pillars of strength. Vulnerabilities, whether they be past traumas, personal insecurities, or emotional sensitivities, are often magnified in relationships with narcissists who prey on perceived weaknesses. The first step toward transformation is identifying these vulnerabilities. Reflect on moments when you felt most hurt or manipulated by someone; these instances often point directly to your emotional vulnerabilities. Whether it's a need for approval that leaves you susceptible to flattery or a fear of rejection that a narcissist can play upon, understanding these triggers is necessary to turn them into strengths.

Once identified, the process of reframing these vulnerabilities begins. The reframing involves a shift in perspective, where you view these traits not as weaknesses but as areas of empowerment. For instance, if sensitivity is your vulnerability, consider how this same sensitivity equips you with the profound capacity for empathy, allowing you to connect with others on a deep emotional level - a strength in both personal relationships and professional environments that value team dynamics and client relations. Similarly, experiences of past trauma can be transformed into a testament to your resilience. These experiences, while challenging, prove your ability to overcome adversity, offering a unique perspective on survival and growth that can inspire and guide others on their journeys.

Protecting these newly reframed vulnerabilities involves setting boundaries that honor your authentic self while preventing narcissistic exploitation, which requires understanding your limits and communicating them clearly in your interactions. Suppose you've identified a tendency to give too much in relationships, leaving you drained. In this case, setting a boundary might involve deciding beforehand how much time and energy you are willing to devote to people, ensuring you conserve enough emotional bandwidth to maintain your well-being. Communicating these boundaries can be challenging, especially with a narcissist who may not respect them. However, consistency in enforcing your limits teaches others how to treat you and signals that your vulnerabilities are not open for exploitation.

Finally, embracing and owning your vulnerabilities as part of your identity is a powerful form of empowerment. This acceptance does not mean resigning yourself to weakness but rather recognizing that these aspects of your character contribute to a fuller, more nuanced self. Owning your story, including the parts shaped by vulnerability, allows you to write the narrative of your life from a place of strength and authenticity. It reframes your past not as a series of events that happened to you but as integral chapters that contributed to your current resilience and depth. This ownership can manifest in various forms, from openly discussing your experiences in supportive settings to using your insights to help others in similar situations. By doing so, you not only affirm the value of your journey but also position your vulnerabilities as sources of strength and wisdom.

Through these strategies, what once might have seemed like your greatest weaknesses can be transformed into your most profound strengths. By identifying, reframing, protecting, and embracing your vulnerabilities, you turn potential points of exploitation into badges of resilience, fundamentally shifting the dynamics of power in your interactions with a narcissist. This process not only safeguards you against manipulation but also enriches your sense of self, grounding your interactions in a deep-seated confidence that is both genuine and unshakeable.

5.4 THE ROLE OF FORGIVENESS: IS IT NECESSARY?

Forgiveness in the context of emotional abuse, particularly when dealing with narcissistic behavior, is a concept that often evokes deep contemplation and mixed emotions. It is not about condoning the actions or absolving the narcissist of their responsibility; rather, it is about releasing the emotional hold that the past has on you. This distinction is crucial in understanding the role of forgiveness on your healing journey. Forgiveness can be seen as a personal process that involves letting go of deep-seated feelings of resentment and anger, which, if held onto, can continue to harm you mentally and emotionally long after the abusive interactions have ended. It's important, however, to recognize that forgiving is not synonymous with forgetting. You can forgive someone and still choose to distance yourself or cut ties to protect your well-being. The act of forgiving can sometimes lead to profound personal growth and emotional relief, but it should never compromise one's sense of safety or self-respect.

The power of forgiveness extends beyond mere emotional relief, as it can significantly affect your mental health. Holding onto anger and resentment can be exhausting and can keep you locked in a cycle of negativity and pain, influencing your overall quality of life. Forgiveness can reduce these distressing emotions, decrease stress, and lead to enhanced psychological well-being. It can also open up space for positive emotions and experiences, allowing for closure on past hurts. It is not about erasing what happened but about changing your relationship with what happened so it no longer controls your emotions or your life. Studies have shown that forgiveness can lead to better cardiovascular health, less anxiety and stress, and higher levels of happiness. It's about reclaiming your power - choosing to no longer be defined by the harm inflicted upon you. It is essential to emphasize that forgiveness is a deeply personal choice and one that should not be rushed or forced. Healing from narcissistic abuse is a complex process that individuals must navigate at their own pace. For some, forgiveness is a crucial step in healing; for others, it may not be necessary or appropriate, depending on the specifics of the abuse and personal values. It's important to honor your feelings and processes, regardless of external expectations or pressures. If forgiveness feels like a step toward freedom, then it may be worth pursuing. However, if the thought of forgiving adds to your stress or feels like a betrayal of your experience, it might not be the right path for you. The goal of healing is not to reach a state of forgiveness but to reach a state of peace and acceptance with your past, whatever it might be.

If you choose to forgive, consider these guidelines to ensure that the process is beneficial and self-affirming. Start by clearly defining what forgiveness means to you and what it does not. Writing a personal forgiveness statement may be helpful. Remember, forgiving does not mean allowing the narcissist back into your life or forgetting the abuse. Next, try to view the situation from a broader perspective. Consider the narcissists' limitations and recognize that their hurtful behaviors reflect their issues, not your worth. This recognition can help reduce personal hurt and facilitate forgiveness. Engage in empathy, not for the narcissist's sake, but for your healing. Understanding that narcissists' harmful actions are driven by their weaknesses can sometimes make forgiveness easier. Lastly, actively choose to let go of the anger and resentment through meditation, therapy, or ritual, like writing a letter of forgiveness you never send. The act of letting go is for you, to free you from the emotional chains that bind you to the past.

In embracing forgiveness, you are not denying the pain caused or the seriousness of the narcissist's behavior. Rather, you are making a powerful decision not to let these experiences dictate your emotional landscape. Whether or not you choose to forgive, the key is to do what feels right for your healing journey, ensuring that any decision to forgive is made for your peace and well-being, not to fulfill an obligation to anyone else. Remember, the path to recovery is uniquely yours, and you have the autonomy to shape it in a way that brings you the most peace, healing, and happiness.

5.5 THE GRAY ROCK METHOD: BECOMING SAFELY BORING

When managing interactions with a narcissist, sometimes the most effective move is to become unremarkably dull - like a gray rock. The Gray Rock Method is a strategic form of interaction that minimizes your responses, making you less appealing and less engaging to a narcissist. This approach is particularly useful in situations where you cannot completely avoid contact but wish to avoid becoming a target of manipulation and emotional drama. By mastering the art of blending in, you reduce the narcissist's interest in you as a source of narcissistic supply - the attention and emotional reactions they thrive on.

Implementing the Gray Rock Method involves a consistent, conscious effort to make your reactions as neutral and uninteresting as possible. Start by moderating your emotional responses. Whether the narcissist tries to bait you with anger, charm, or guilt, your job is to respond with evasive answers like "Hmm," "I see," or "Okay." Avoid sharing personal stories, feelings, or anything that might pique the narcissist's interest or give him/her ammunition to manipulate you later. For example, if the narcissist tries to engage you in a heated debate or pry into your personal life, steer the conversation towards mundane topics, like the weather or your neutral plans for the weekend. The key is to keep your interactions as brief and impersonal as possible.

Practicing this method can be challenging, especially at first. It may feel unnatural or even rude to withhold your natural reactions and emotions. Role-playing can be an invaluable tool in this regard. With a trusted friend or therapist, simulate interactions where you practice being a 'gray rock.' These role-plays can help you get used to delivering flat, unemotional responses, even when provoked. They also provide a safe space to refine your approach based on feedback, ensuring that when you use this method in real situations, it feels more comfortable and effective.

However, while the Gray Rock Method can be a powerful tool, you should be aware of its challenges and limitations. One of the most significant challenges is maintaining this approach consistently, especially during prolonged exposure to the narcissist. It can be mentally exhausting to suppress your natural reactions continually and maintain a facade of dullness. Moreover, if the narcissist senses your strategy, they might escalate their efforts to provoke a reaction, which can be incredibly stressful and emotionally taxing.

The effectiveness and safety of the Gray Rock Method depend largely on the specific dynamics of your relationship with the narcissist. It is most effective in situations where direct and complete cutting of ties is not possible, such as when co-parenting or in a professional environment. In these scenarios, reducing your emotional and informational output can minimize conflict and emotional abuse. However, it's crucial to monitor the effect of this method on your mental health. Continually suppressing your emotions can lead to feelings of isolation, depression, or loss of self. It's important to have support systems in place, such as friends, family, or a therapist, to whom you can express your feelings and experiences openly and safely.

In conclusion, while the Gray Rock Method can serve as a protective measure in dealing with a narcissist, it should be used judiciously and with an awareness of the potential emotional cost. Balancing this strategy with outlets for emotional expression and support ensures that you remain healthy and resilient, preserving your well-being while navigating the challenging waters of interaction with a narcissist.

5.6 INTUITION AND ITS ROLE IN PREDICTING MANIPULATIVE BEHAVIOR

Intuition, often referred to as a 'gut feeling,' is an intrinsic and powerful tool, particularly when navigating the murky waters of relationships infused with narcissism. This internal compass, when finely tuned, can alert you to subtleties that might not be immediately obvious, guiding you away from potential emotional traps set by manipulative individuals. Strengthening your intuition is not just about honing an instinct; it is about aligning your emotional perception with experiential learning to form a protective barrier against manipulation.

Enhancing your intuition involves a blend of mindfulness, reflective practices, and an honest evaluation of past interactions. Regular meditation can serve as a grounding technique, quieting the noise of daily life and allowing you to connect more deeply with your subconscious mind. This connection is crucial, as intuition often speaks in whispers, not shouts. Cultivating a state of calm through meditation allows you to become more attuned to these whispers, which can warn you of incongruences in a narcissist's words and actions. Additionally, reflective journaling acts as a mirror to your experiences, helping you document and interpret your emotional reactions and thoughts about past interactions. Over time, this journal becomes a valuable resource, revealing patterns and red flags that you might have previously overlooked.

Learning from your experiences is integral to strengthening your intuitive sense. Each interaction, whether positive or negative, holds valuable lessons. By actively reflecting on what felt 'off' in previous encounters with manipulative individuals, you begin to identify specific behaviors that triggered discomfort or doubt, such as an inconsistency in their story, an unexplained shift in their demeanor, or perhaps a subtle dismissal of your feelings. Recognizing these signs sharpens your intuitive ability to detect similar red flags in future interactions, enhancing your protective instincts.

Trusting your gut is sometimes easier said than done, especially in environments where manipulation has previously clouded your judgment. However, the more you honor these instinctual feelings, whether they urge caution or encourage openness, the stronger and more reliable they become. Trusting your intuition means listening to that inner voice when it tells you something isn't right, even if everything appears perfect on the surface. It's about respecting your feelings and allowing them to guide you, particularly in relationships where past manipulation has eroded your trust in your perceptions.

Balancing intuition with rational thought is the key to ensuring that your decisions are comprehensive and grounded. While intuition can alert you to potential red flags, rational thought provides a logical framework for interpreting these feelings. It's a symbiotic relationship in that your intuition might sense a discrepancy in someone's words while your rational mind will analyze the context, the possible motivations behind their words, and the implications of their actions. This balance prevents you from swinging too far towards paranoia or naivety, enabling you to make decisions that are both emotionally and logically sound.

Integrating these elements fosters a robust sense of intuition that shields and guides your interactions with narcissists. By strengthening your intuition, recognizing the subtle cues that signal manipulative behavior, trusting your gut reactions, and balancing these insights with rational analysis, you equip yourself with a nuanced understanding of human behavior. This understanding not only protects you but also empowers you to navigate complex social landscapes with confidence and clarity.

Reflecting on the journey through this chapter, we've explored the profound role of intuition in recognizing and thwarting manipulative behaviors. By honing this intuitive sense, you've gained an invaluable ally in your ongoing interactions not just with narcissists but in all areas of your life where authenticity and honesty are paramount. As we turn the page to the next chapter, we'll build on these insights, focusing on proactive strategies to further safeguard your emotional health and enhance your interpersonal engagements.

CHAPTER 6

STRATEGIES FOR COUNTER-MANIPULATION

I magine standing at the edge of a labyrinth, where the whims of a narcissist dictate each turn and twist. Navigating this maze requires more than just awareness; it demands a proactive stance, a strategic mindset, and, above all, the ability to set and maintain boundaries that shield your emotional well-being. This chapter is about transforming insight into action, equipping you with the tools to not just survive but reclaim control in relationships dominated by narcissistic dynamics. Here, the focus shifts from understanding to action, from awareness to application, ensuring that you are prepared to stand your ground and preserve your integrity against the manipulative onslaughts of a narcissist.

6.1 SETTING BOUNDARIES: TECHNIQUES AND ASSERTIVE COMMUNICATION

Setting boundaries is akin to drawing a map of your territory; it involves defining where you end, and someone else begins. In relationships with narcissists, who often see others as extensions of themselves rather than as separate individuals with distinct needs, establishing clear personal and emotional boundaries is crucial. These boundaries can vary significantly, from deciding not to discuss certain topics that lead to manipulation to limiting the amount of time you spend in the narcissist's presence. For example, you might decide that conversations about your career are off-limits if your narcissistic partner tends to belittle your accomplishments. Or perhaps you choose to limit personal interactions to public spaces where the narcissist is less likely to exhibit controlling or demeaning behavior.

Assertiveness is the key to communicating these boundaries effectively. It is about being direct and honest about your needs and feelings without being aggressive or confrontational. This distinction is crucial; whereas aggression attacks, assertiveness respects both your rights and those of others. Effective assertive communication involves using "I" statements that focus on your feelings and needs rather than on criticizing or blaming the other person. For instance, saying, "I feel overwhelmed when we discuss my job, so I'd like to focus on other topics," clearly communicates your boundary without attacking the other person's character.

Role-Playing Scenarios: Practicing Boundary Setting

To build confidence in setting and communicating boundaries, role-playing can be an invaluable tool. Engaging in role-playing scenarios with friends or therapists allows you to practice how to respond to different situations in a safe environment. These exercises can help you refine your wording, tone, and body language, making it easier to transfer these skills into real-life interactions. For instance, you might role-play a scenario where the narcissist criticizes you in public. Practicing how to calmly communicate that this behavior is unacceptable and that you will remove yourself from the situation if it continues helps prepare you to act decisively in real situations.

Handling boundary violations is another critical aspect of dealing with narcissists. It is not uncommon for narcissists to test or even disregard set boundaries, requiring you to be prepared to reinforce them consistently. When a boundary is crossed, it is important to respond immediately and firmly, reiterating the boundary and the consequences if it continues to be disregarded. Phrases like, "As I mentioned before, I will not discuss this topic. If you continue, I will need to end our conversation," can be effective. This consistent reinforcement makes it clear that you are serious about your boundaries and are prepared to take action to protect them.

Setting and maintaining boundaries with a narcissist can be challenging but is essential for protecting your emotional health and ensuring your interactions are based on respect and equality. Through assertive communication, role-playing practice, and consistent reinforcement, you can establish a framework that not only defends against narcissistic manipulation but also empowers you to lead a more autonomous and fulfilling life.

6.2 THE ART OF DISENGAGEMENT: KNOWING WHEN TO WALK AWAY

Navigating through the turbulent waters of a relationship with a narcissist often means recognizing when the costs begin to outweigh the benefits, a realization that can be as painful as it is necessary. Understanding when and how to disengage from interactions with a narcissist is vital to preserving your mental and emotional health. Sometimes, the most powerful move is to step back, especially when dealing with unproductive or harmful scenarios that a narcissist often orchestrates. The art of disengagement isn't about giving up or conceding defeat; rather, it's about taking control of your life and conserving your energy for healthier, more constructive relationships.

Understand to Anticipate

Recognizing unwinnable situations is the first step toward effective disengagement. A situation is typically deemed unwinnable when any form of engagement does not change the outcome and continues to cause you emotional pain or stress. These are scenarios where the narcissist uses every opportunity to belittle, confuse, or manipulate you. For instance, if discussions about plans always end in arguments or if your accomplishments are constantly undermined, these are clear indicators that the interaction is likely to be detrimental. The goal here is not to win against the narcissist but to protect your well-being. Identifying these patterns allows you to make informed decisions about when to engage and when it's best to step away.

Disengaging tactically involves a mixture of foresight, calmness, and resolution. One approach is using neutral statements that neither provoke further conflict nor invite additional conversation. Phrases like "I see your point" or "Let's talk about this later" can be useful. Physically removing yourself from a toxic situation can also be a necessary and clear-cut method of disengagement. This might mean walking out of a room, ending a phone call, or even leaving a social event early. The key is to do so calmly and without showing signs of agitation, which might provide the narcissist with more ammunition to use against you in the future. By managing your exit gracefully, you signal that you are in control of your actions and emotions, not the narcissist.

Emotional Detachment Techniques

Detaching emotionally from a narcissist is crucial during the disengagement process, as it prevents their actions from impacting their emotional state. Techniques such as deep breathing, mindfulness, and focusing on logical, factual aspects of the interaction can help maintain your mental focus. For example, if a narcissist begins a tirade, you might choose to focus on a physical object in the room, count backward from 100, or plan your activities for the next day in your head. These tactics help create emotional distance and prevent the narcissist from drawing you into their emotional drama. Remember, the goal of emotional detachment is not to feel less but to manage your feelings in ways that protect your emotional stability.

Long-term disengagement from a narcissist, especially if the relationship is a significant one like a marriage or a long-term partnership, requires careful planning and consideration. Start by gradually reducing your emotional and physical availability. Communicate more via text or email rather than in-person conversations, as this can help minimize direct manipulation. Begin to build a support network outside of the relationship, including friends, family, or professional counselors who understand your situation and can offer practical advice and emotional support. If the decision is to end the relationship entirely, consider all practical implications, such as living arrangements, financial matters, and co-parenting if children are involved. Each step should be planned methodically, ideally with the support of legal or psychological professionals, to ensure that you are protected throughout the process.

Disengaging from a narcissist, whether temporarily or permanently, is an act of self-preservation. It involves recognizing harmful situations, employing tactics to reduce conflict, detaching emotionally, and planning for long-term separation if necessary. These steps are designed not only to protect your emotional and mental health but also to empower you to lead a life defined by respectful and supportive relationships. Taking control in this way can be one of the most liberating steps you take on your path to recovery and personal growth.

6.3 VERBAL SELF-DEFENSE TACTICS: WORDS THAT DISARM

In the complex dance of verbal exchanges with a narcissist, the words you choose and how you deliver them can significantly alter the dynamics of the conversation. This is not about outsmarting or defeating the narcissist verbally but about protecting your mental space and maintaining control over the interaction. It begins with the strategic use of non-combative language, a tool that can defuse potential conflicts and keep the conversation from escalating. Non-combative language involves phrases and tones that express your points without aggression, maintaining a calm and clear manner of speaking. For instance, instead of saying, "You always ignore my needs," you could express, "I feel overlooked when my needs aren't considered." This subtle shift in phrasing can prevent the narcissist from becoming defensive and, more likely, keeps the discussion productive.

One effective strategy is redirecting conversations, which involves steering the dialogue away from topics that might trigger manipulative behavior or areas where the narcissist seeks control. This technique requires you to be both alert and creative, recognizing when the conversation is veering into dangerous waters and knowing how to subtly change its course. If a narcissist begins to pry into personal matters that are off-limits, you might redirect by bringing up a neutral topic or asking the narcissist a question about their interests, something that narcissists often can't resist. For example, if the conversation starts to turn towards criticisms of your family, you could interject with, "Speaking of families, didn't you mention a family reunion you're planning? How is that going?" This not only shifts the focus but also engages the narcissist in a safer, less charged topic.

Another crucial element of verbal self-defense is tactical ignoring. This involves choosing to ignore or not respond to certain provocations or manipulative comments. Narcissists often use provocative statements to elicit an emotional reaction that they can then exploit. By selectively ignoring these provocations, you deny them the reaction they seek, which can diminish their power in the interaction. It's important to differentiate this from passive behavior; tactical ignoring is a deliberate choice to not engage with specific comments that serve no purpose other than to manipulate or upset you. For example, if a narcissist makes an offhand remark meant to bait you into an argument or make you feel guilty, maintaining your focus on the topic at hand or even remaining silent can serve as a powerful countermeasure.

Assertive responses are also key in maintaining your ground without escalating the situation. This involves recognizing common narcissistic tactics like gaslighting or guilt-tripping and responding in a way that is both firm and composed. When confronted with gaslighting, where the narcissist might deny your experience or reality, a response such as, "I acknowledge your perspective, but my experience was quite different," helps validate your perceptions without directly challenging theirs. In cases of guilt-tripping, a response like, "I understand you're upset, and I'm sorry you feel that way, but this decision is important for my well-being," can affirm your actions without succumbing to emotional manipulation. These responses require not just an understanding of what is being said but also why it's being said, allowing you to address the underlying manipulation rather than just the surface words.

Mastering these verbal self-defense tactics empowers you to navigate conversations with a narcissist with greater confidence and control. By using non-combative language, redirecting conversations, tactically ignoring provocations, and crafting assertive responses, you create a repertoire of strategies that protect your interests and maintain your emotional balance. These techniques not only help in managing interactions with a narcissist but also enhance your communication skills in all areas of life, leading to more respectful and productive dialogues.

6.4 MAINTAINING COMPOSURE UNDER ATTACK: PRACTICAL EXERCISES

When faced with the escalating pressures of a confrontation, especially one steered by a narcissist, maintaining your composure is both a shield and a strategy. It's about holding your ground in the face of emotional barrages, preserving your mental clarity, and responding in a way that reflects your integrity, not your impulse. The ability to stay composed under attack doesn't just happen - it's a skill honed through deliberate practice and preparation. This section explores practical exercises designed to strengthen your composure, providing you with the tools to remain calm and collected, no matter the emotional turbulence you may encounter.

Breathing techniques serve as a foundational tool in this arsenal. The simple act of controlled breathing can have a profound impact on your ability to stay calm under pressure. One effective method is the 4-7-8 breathing technique, which involves breathing in for four seconds, holding the breath for seven seconds, and exhaling slowly for eight seconds. This exercise helps regulate your heart rate and directs your focus away from the stressor, anchoring you in the present moment and reducing physiological symptoms of stress. Imagine you are in the midst of a heated exchange where a narcissist is attempting to provoke you by undermining your contributions in a team meeting. By discreetly practicing this breathing technique, you can maintain your calm, think more clearly, and respond from a place of composure rather than react impulsively.

Visualization is another powerful technique that prepares you to handle confrontations without losing your composure. This involves creating a detailed mental image of the challenging situation and seeing yourself handling it with calm and confidence. Before an anticipated difficult interaction, take a moment to close your eyes and vividly imagine the scenario. Picture the setting, the people involved, and the potential triggers. Then, visualize yourself responding with calmness and assertiveness - your voice steady, your posture relaxed, your breathing even. The more detailed the visualization, the better prepared you will feel. This mental rehearsal builds a psychological blueprint, which can guide your actions during the actual confrontation, making you less likely to be swept away by emotions.

Physical Anchors for Calm

Physical anchors act as subtle yet powerful reminders to maintain composure. These can be simple physical actions like pressing your fingers together, touching a piece of jewelry, or gently tapping your foot on the floor. These actions serve as cues to breathe, reflect, and respond thoughtfully rather than succumbing to emotional reactions. During interactions where you feel your stress levels rising, these physical anchors can bring you back to a state of calm. For example, if, during a discussion, a narcissist starts attacking your decisions, you might gently press your thumb and forefinger together under the table. This action serves as a cue to initiate deep breathing, helping you to maintain your composure and address the situation calmly.

Rehearsal and preparation are crucial in solidifying these techniques into your behavioral response patterns. Regularly practicing these exercises, both in everyday situations and before anticipated difficult interactions, builds familiarity and confidence. Set aside a few minutes each day to practice breathing exercises, engage in visualization, and establish your physical anchors. Over time, these practices become ingrained, automatically activating in situations where you need them most. Additionally, consider scenarios where you might face criticism or emotional manipulation and rehearse how you would employ these techniques. The more you practice, the more intuitive your composure will become, transforming your ability to handle confrontations with grace and effectiveness.

By integrating these practical exercises into your routine, you equip yourself with a robust set of tools that enhance your ability to maintain composure in the face of narcissistic attacks. These techniques not only prepare you to manage stress and conflict more effectively but also empower you to navigate your interactions with a sense of control and self-assurance. Through regular practice and application, you can transform composure from a temporary state to a lasting trait, one that fortifies your interactions and upholds your dignity, no matter the challenges you face.

6.5 LEVERAGING SILENCE: WHEN NOT TO ENGAGE

Silence, often overlooked, holds a profound power in conversations, especially when dealing with someone as manipulatively vocal as a narcissist. While it might seem counterintuitive, choosing not to respond can sometimes be the most powerful statement you can make. Silence isn't just the absence of speech; it's a strategic tool that can shift the dynamics of interaction, often leading the narcissist to reveal more about their intentions and weaknesses without you having to utter a single word. When a narcissist expects a reaction - whether defensive, submissive, or combative - opting to remain silent can disrupt their strategy, forcing them to expose their tactics or become unnerved by the lack of expected feedback. This shift can provide you with valuable insights into their behavior, motivations, and potential next moves, positioning you to better manage the interaction on your terms.

The strategic use of silence involves understanding when it is most effective. It works particularly well in situations where any verbal response would likely escalate the conflict or when the narcissist is fishing for emotional reactions to use against you. For instance, if a narcissist dramatically criticizes your work in a meeting to provoke insecurity or anger, responding might lead you into a defensive stance, which the narcissist could exploit to undermine your credibility further. In contrast, by remaining silent, you retain control over your emotions and deny the narcissist the response they seek, often leading them to overextend or repeat themselves, which can reveal to observers the narcissist's true nature.

Silence should not be misconstrued as passivity but rather seen as a form of assertive non-engagement. By choosing silence, you are actively deciding that this is not a battle worth your energy or that engaging verbally does not serve your interests. This decision is a strong assertion of your boundaries and an expression of control over the situation. It communicates that you are not easily swayed by attempts to unsettle or manipulate you, enhancing your position of strength. Moreover, silence can be a clear indicator of dissent or disapproval, as potent as words but without the potential repercussions of an emotional or aggressive verbal exchange.

The impact of your silence on a narcissist can be significant. Narcissists thrive on the verbal reactions they can provoke. Your silence can lead to frustration, confusion, or even anger on their part, as it deprives them of the feedback loop necessary to gauge and manipulate your emotions. In many cases, this can lead them to change tactics, often making errors or revealing inconsistencies in their arguments as they struggle to regain control of the dialogue. Observing these changes can provide critical insights into their strategy and personality, allowing you to plan your responses in future interactions more effectively. Silence, therefore, not only serves as a shield protecting you from immediate emotional harm but also as a lens, sharpening your focus on the narcissist's behavior and tactics.

In embracing silence, you harness a subtle yet powerful tool that enhances your strategic repertoire in dealing with narcissists. This approach allows you to conserve your emotional resources, gather intelligence on the narcissist's behavior, and assert your autonomy in the relationship, all without saying a word. As you continue to navigate these complex dynamics, remember that silence, when used judiciously, is not just a passive state but an active strategy, empowering you to control the narrative and protect your mental and emotional well-being.

6.6 ANTICIPATING MOVES: THINKING LIKE A CHESS PLAYER

In the intricate game of dealing with a narcissist, understanding their typical behavioral patterns and tactics is akin to a chess player who not only knows the rules but also reads the opponent's strategies. Narcissists often follow predictable patterns, including idealization followed by devaluation, as well as tactics such as gaslighting, guilt-tripping, and creating emotional confusion. Recognizing these patterns is crucial because it enhances your ability to anticipate what moves the narcissist might make next. Just as a skilled chess player looks several moves ahead, anticipating a narcissist's actions allows you to prepare and strategize effectively. For example, if you notice the initial signs of idealization, where the narcissist showers you with praise and attention, you can predict that this might eventually transition to devaluation, preparing you to safeguard your emotions and responses.

Strategic planning, then, involves not just recognizing these patterns but also formulating a plan based on this understanding. This includes deciding in advance how to respond to potential manipulations, what boundaries to enforce, and when to disengage. Think of it as setting up your chess pieces in defensive positions; you are less likely to be caught off guard and more likely to maintain control of the game. For instance, if you anticipate that a discussion might lead to narcissistic rage, planning to remain calm and using techniques like tactical ignoring can help you manage the situation more effectively. This strategic planning isn't about manipulating the narcissist in return but about protecting your own mental and emotional well-being.

Adapting strategies based on feedback is also essential. Just as a chess player might alter their strategy based on the moves their opponent makes, you should be prepared to adjust your responses based on the narcissist's actions. This dynamic approach allows you to remain flexible and responsive. If, for example, you find that a particular response tends to escalate conflicts rather than de-escalate them, it might be wise to try a different approach. This could involve changing the way you communicate your boundaries or finding new ways to assert your needs without confrontation. Keeping a mental or even physical journal of interactions can help track what works and what doesn't, providing a practical feedback loop that informs your strategy.

Maintaining emotional distance is perhaps one of the most challenging yet vital aspects of engaging with a narcissist, especially if the interactions are frequent or the relationship is significant, such as a family member or a workplace supervisor. This doesn't mean you don't care; rather, it's about protecting your inner self from the emotional turmoil that such interactions can often stir up. Emotional detachment requires practice and mindfulness; it involves observing the interactions as if you were a third party, recognizing the tactics being used, and consciously choosing not to let them affect your emotional state. Techniques such as focusing on factual information rather than emotional content, practicing mindfulness to stay anchored in the present moment, and engaging in regular mental health practices like meditation or therapy can all support this emotional distancing. By maintaining a clear emotional boundary, you preserve your mental clarity and focus, which is essential for navigating complex interactions with a narcissist without losing sight of your own needs and well-being.

In summary, thinking like a chess player when dealing with a narcissist involves understanding and anticipating their moves, strategically planning your responses, adapting your tactics based on what is effective, and maintaining emotional distance to protect your mental focus. These strategies empower you to manage interactions with narcissists proactively and healthily, ensuring that you remain in control of your emotions and responses rather than being manipulated or hurt by theirs.

As we close this chapter on counter-manipulation strategies, remember that dealing with a narcissist, much like playing chess, requires patience, strategy, and a clear understanding of the opponent's tactics. Each technique and approach discussed not only enhances your ability to handle interactions with narcissists but also strengthens your overall interpersonal skills, making you more adept at navigating a variety of challenging social situations. Moving forward, the next chapter will delve into the nuances of healing and recovery, guiding you through the process of rebuilding your sense of self and emotional health after experiencing narcissistic abuse. This next step, while challenging, is crucial for regaining your independence and moving towards a more fulfilling life.

CHAPTER 7
PSEUDO-AGREEMENT AS A COUNTER MANIPULATION TACTIC

In the intricate dance of human communication, the ways in which people express agreement and disagreement can significantly impact relationships and interactions. One particularly insidious form of communication is "pseudo-agreeing" - a behavior where individuals appear to agree with others superficially while holding differing opinions or intentions beneath the surface. Thus, by agreeing with your partner or a colleague, you disarm them immediately. Imagine your husband is trying to manipulate you - he wants to scare you and says, "We don't get along with each other. Let's divorce!" Just say, "Ok," and he's got no more cards to play. Of course, he might make another attempt and say, for example, "Good! So when are you moving out?" Just say, "Whenever you want" Or, imagine, your boss called you a stupid and unprofessional individual. Instead of trying to prove to him that he is wrong, say, "Yes. I understand your position". The manipulated doesn't mean what he says, but he wants you to react, to begin apologizing, explaining, arguing... Do what they expect you to. Disarm them with a pseudo-agreement, show them that their trick doesn't work, and next time, they might not use this stacking tactic against you.

This chapter explores the concept of pseudo-agreeing, its implications in various contexts, and strategies to recognize and address it effectively. We will discuss how pseudo-agreement can serve as a counter-manipulation strategy, allowing individuals to navigate tricky relational dynamics without escalating conflict or sacrificing their integrity.

7.1 UNDERSTANDING PSEUDO-AGREEING

Manipulation occurs when one party attempts to control or influence another's thoughts or behaviors for personal gain, often at the expense of the other person's well-being. This can manifest through tactics such as guilt-tripping, gaslighting, or passive-aggressive behavior. Understanding the dynamics of manipulation is crucial to recognizing when it occurs and formulating an appropriate response.

Pseudo-agreement can serve as a strategic tool in countering manipulation. By seemingly agreeing with the manipulator, the individual can defuse tension, buy time to assess the situation, and ultimately regain a sense of control. This approach can be particularly effective when confrontation might escalate the situation or when the manipulative behavior is subtle and hard to address head-on.

Agreeing in a noncommittal way can help to diffuse the manipulator's emotional intensity. Instead of escalating the conflict, the individual can redirect the conversation or change the subject, reducing the pressure.

While a manipulator seeks to exert control, pseudo-agreement allows the individual to retain a sense of agency. They can choose when and how to engage more deeply with the issue at hand.

Agreeing can also serve as a tactic to gather more information about the manipulative behavior. By maintaining a calm facade, the individual can observe the manipulator's reactions and motivations without revealing their stance or intentions.

Besides, by agreeing superficially, the individual can create a buffer that allows them to step back from the immediate emotional charge of the conversation. This distance can provide clarity and prevent knee-jerk reactions.

7.2 HOW PSEUDO-AGREEING WORKS

People often engage in pseudo-agreeing to sidestep uncomfortable discussions or potential confrontations, and this is the best tactic to avoid conflict. Especially when you know you might have a bad consequence, or you understand that your partner is seeking for the argument.

While appearing agreeable to a Narcissist externally internally, you may feel frustrated, misunderstood, or even hostile. But don't show it. Instead, show your opponent that his manipulation doesn't work. Put a poker face on and agree. You'll see the results very quickly, and you will be astonished at how well this tactic works against all sorts of manipulations.

Remember, pseudo-agreeing is just a strategic maneuver. Some of you would say, "I can not agree when my husband insults me," or "I can not accept that my boss thinks I'm unprofessional." But in fact, if you are dealing with a narcissist, all they want is to make you react, gain favor, control, or achieve a personal agenda, and that's their way of doing it. Pseudo-agreeing is no more than a shield against Manipulative Intentions.

Imagine a scenario where a friend consistently makes remarks about feeling abandoned because you spend time with other friends. Rather than confronting them directly, you might say, "I understand you feel that way; I'll try to make more time for you." This pseudo-agreement acknowledges their feelings without committing to a course of action that could further entrap them in their guilt-tripping behavior.

Or, in a relationship, your partner may say, "If you really loved me, you would do this for me." Instead of reacting defensively, you might respond, "I see your point; we need to support each other." This allows you to acknowledge their feelings while also deflecting the manipulative intent behind their statement. Later, you can address the underlying issue more constructively.

7.3 THE CONSEQUENCES OF PSEUDO-AGREEING: BE AWARE OF WHOM YOU ARE DEALING WITH

While pseudo-agreeing may provide short-term relief from conflict, it can lead to a variety of long-term consequences, and that is why it is so important to be able to recognize a Narcissist and understand whom you are dealing with.

When we are dealing with "normal" people, agreeing without agreeing can lead to erosion of trust. When individuals discover that someone has been insincerely agreeing with them, it can lead to feelings of betrayal and distrust. But when we deal with a Narcissist - pseudo-agreeing becomes a counter-manipulative technique, which intends to prevent further manipulations on their behalf.

In interactions with "normal" people, Pseudo-agreeing stifles genuine dialogue, preventing the resolution of underlying issues and leading to misunderstandings. Again, be aware of whom you are dealing with. This book is about counter-manipulating a narcissist, and it may always be suitable with ordinary people who are seeking a real conflict resolution when the internal conflict of agreeing while disagreeing can lead to pent-up frustration and resentment, causing emotional distance in relationships.

7.4 RECOGNIZING PSEUDO-AGREEING

To navigate the complexities of communication effectively, you need to be able to recognize when pseudo-agreeing occurs against you. Here are some signs to look for:

Pay attention to nonverbal cues such as crossed arms, lack of eye contact, or facial expressions that contradict verbal agreement. Learn to read a body language.

Pseudo-agreeing often involves non-committal language and vague responses, such as "I guess that makes sense" or "Sure, if you think so," which lacks genuine enthusiasm or conviction.

An insincere agreement may be accompanied by a flat or sarcastic tone, indicating a lack of true support or belief.

If someone agrees but then fails to engage further in the conversation, doesn't pose any follow-up questions, or shifts the topic quickly, it may signal that their agreement is not genuine.

7.5 STRATEGIES TO ADDRESS PSEUDO-AGREEING WHILE DEALING WITH A NARCISSIST

When it comes to dealing with narcissists, pseudo-agreement might become their means to neglect you and your feelings. They don't want to engage in conflict resolution, and they avoid it by all means. For them, conflict is there to stay, and that's their way to maintain control over you.

When you feel your narcissist applies pseudo-agreement while you are trying to encourage an open dialogue, you can confront them by asking clarifying questions. Ask them to elaborate on their thoughts. Questions such as "What do you think about that?" can prompt deeper reflection. Encourage them to share their "true" opinions and listen carefully to what they say. At some point, they will involuntarily reveal their true attitude towards the subject. Narcissists generally like attention. They love to speak.

Another piece of advice - remain clear on your positions and beliefs. Stay Grounded in Reality. Document conversations if necessary so you have a reference point for future discussions. Always focus on Facts. Emphasize objective facts and data in discussions. This can help minimize emotional manipulation and encourage more rational dialogue.

Clearly define what behaviors are acceptable and what are not. If the pseudo-agreement leads to manipulation or gaslighting, assertively communicate your boundaries.

Use "I" Statements to frame your feelings and thoughts in a way that emphasizes your perspective. For example, say "I feel that..." instead of "You should...". This can make it harder for them to dismiss your concerns.

Understand that their behavior is a reflection of their personality and not a measure of their worth or validity in the conversation. Try to Avoid Personalization.

Try to Stay Calm and Composed. Narcissists often thrive on emotional reactions. Keeping your composure can prevent them from gaining the upper hand in the conversation.

If possible, Limit Engagement. When the pseudo-agreement becomes a pattern that frustrates you, consider limiting your interactions with the individual, especially for topics that lead to conflict.

When you challenge a narcissist's behavior or call out pseudo-agreement, be prepared for potential retaliation or further manipulation. Stay firm in your stance.

Pseudo-agreement can be a valuable counter-manipulation strategy in navigating complex relational dynamics. By employing this technique thoughtfully, individuals can create space for honest dialogue and reduce the emotional charge of manipulative interactions. However, it is crucial to recognize the limits of pseudo-agreement and transition to more authentic communication practices to foster trust, respect, and emotional connection in relationships.

As we navigate the complexities of human interaction, let us strive for authenticity, embracing the discomfort that may come with honest conversations. By doing so, we can cultivate relation-ships that are not only resilient to manipulation but also rich in understanding, empathy, and mutual support. Ultimately, the goal is to create a healthy relational environment where all parties can thrive, feel valued, and grow together.

CHAPTER 8
REFRAMING AS A COUNTER MANIPULATION TACTIC

M anipulation often lurks in the shadows, seeking to exploit vulnerabilities and sway opinions. Whether in personal relationships, corporate environments, or even casual conversations, the ability to recognize and counteract manipulation is essential for maintaining autonomy and fostering healthy communication. One of the most powerful tools at our disposal is reframing - a technique that allows us to shift perspectives and redefine narratives to regain control over our interactions.

Reframing, as a method of counter-manipulation, involves shifting the perspective or interpretation of a situation to influence how others perceive it. This technique can be particularly useful in negotiations, conflict resolution, and interpersonal communications, where one party may attempt to manipulate perceptions or emotions to gain an advantage. Here's how reframing can be applied as a counter-manipulation strategy.

8.1 UNDERSTANDING MANIPULATION

Before we dive into the mechanics of reframing, it's crucial to understand what manipulation looks like, whether it is in the form of guilt-tripping, fear-mongering, gaslighting, or even subtle coercion. If one party uses emotional or psychological tactics to elicit a desired response from another - it is manipulation. Recognizing these tactics is the first step in disarming them.

Consider a scenario: during a team meeting, your colleague insists that if you don't support their proposal, the project will fail. This statement is laden with emotional pressure, aiming to evoke fear and guilt. In such moments, your ability to reframe the narrative can not only protect you from undue influence but also redirect the conversation toward a more constructive outcome.

8.2 THE MECHANICS OF REFRAMING

Reframing involves altering the context or interpretation of a situation, allowing you to view it from a new angle. This shift can transform how both you and the other party perceive the issue at hand. Here's how to effectively employ reframing as a counter-manipulation strategy.

Start by pinpointing the core message being conveyed. What are the emotional triggers at play? Understanding the underlying narrative is crucial for effective reframing.

In the heat of manipulation, responses can be knee-jerk reactions. Take a moment to breathe and reflect on your response. This pause allows you to gather your thoughts and approach the situation with a clearer mindset.

Instead of engaging with the manipulative statement directly, redirect the conversation toward a broader context. For instance, respond with, "I understand your concerns about project success. Let's discuss how we can collectively ensure that we meet our goals."

Reframing isn't just about countering negativity; it's also about highlighting potential benefits. If someone is framing a situation in a way that emphasizes risk, respond by identifying potential opportunities for growth or learning.

The words we choose can significantly impact the emotional tone of a conversation. By employing positive language, you can transform a confrontational dialogue into a collaborative discussion. Instead of saying, "I can't agree with your approach," try, "I see where you're coming from, but I believe we could enhance our strategy by considering a different angle."

Sometimes, simply acknowledging the other person's feelings can open the door to a more constructive dialogue. You might say, "I hear that you're worried about the outcome, and that's valid. Let's explore how we can address those concerns together."

Reframing isn't just a defensive tactic; it can also foster a sense of collaboration. By inviting others to participate in finding solutions, you create an atmosphere of teamwork rather than tension.

Let's consider a real-world example. Imagine you're in a negotiation for a pay raise. Your manager insists that the budget is tight and that any increase would jeopardize team resources. This statement is a classic manipulation tactic designed to make you feel guilty for wanting more.

Instead of consenting to the pressure, you might respond with a reframed perspective: "I understand that budget constraints are a challenge. However, I believe that investing in my role could actually lead to increased productivity and innovation within the team. Can we explore how a raise might enhance my contributions?"

In this example, you've shifted the focus from limitations to potential benefits, thereby reframing the conversation in a way that encourages dialogue rather than defensiveness.

Mastering the art of reframing empowers you to navigate the complexities of human interaction with confidence and clarity. By recognizing manipulation and employing reframing techniques, you not only protect your autonomy but also create opportunities for constructive dialogue. In a world where persuasion and influence are ubiquitous, the ability to reframe can be a game-changer, leading to healthier relationships, more effective communication, and, ultimately, better outcomes for all parties involved.

As we continue our exploration of interpersonal dynamics, remember that every conversation is an opportunity to wield the power of reframing. By embracing this technique, you can transform challenges into opportunities, ensuring that you remain in control of

Example of Reframing as a Counter-Manipulation in a Romantic Relationship

Imagine a scenario when your partner expresses frustration over your spending habits, saying something like, "You're so irresponsible with money! If you keep this up, we'll never be able to save for our future together."

Manipulative Statement:

"You're so irresponsible with money! If you keep this up, we'll never be able to save for our future together."

This statement is accusatory and uses fear of the future to manipulate your feelings, making you feel guilty and defensive.

Reframed Response:

To counter this manipulation, you can reframe the conversation to shift the focus from blame to understanding and constructive discussion. Here's how you might respond:

"I appreciate your concern about our financial future, and I want us to be on the same page. Instead of focusing on what I might be doing wrong, let's look at our financial goals together. What specific savings targets do you have in mind, and how can we create a plan that works for both of us?"

Breakdown of the Reframed Response:

You start by acknowledging your partner's concern, which shows that you value their perspective.

By reframing the focus from "irresponsibility" to "financial goals," you change the narrative from a personal attack to a shared objective. This helps reduce defensiveness and opens up the conversation.

Asking for specific savings targets encourages your partner to articulate their concerns constructively. It shifts the discussion from emotional reactions to practical planning.

By suggesting that you create a plan together, you foster a sense of teamwork rather than an adversarial relationship. This collaborative approach helps both partners feel invested in the outcome.

This reframed response not only diffuses the emotional charge of the original statement but also transforms the conversation into a productive dialogue about shared goals. It allows both partners to express their concerns and work together towards a common vision for their future rather than getting caught up in accusations and defensiveness.

In love relationships, reframing can be a powerful counter-manipulation technique. By shifting the focus from blame and fear to collaboration and understanding, you can create a healthier dialogue that fosters connection and mutual support. This approach not only helps resolve conflicts but also strengthens the relationship by promoting open communication and shared goals.

CHAPTER 9
CONCRETIZATION: A SHIELD AGAINST MANIPULATION

In the realm of interpersonal communication and negotiation, manipulation often relies on vague language, emotional appeals, and ambiguous statements to exert influence over others. Concretization techniques involve making abstract concepts more tangible and specific. In the context of navigating conflicts with narcissists, these techniques can provide clarity, focus, and structure to your interactions to enhance the Aikido approach. Concretization can help you articulate your thoughts clearly, set boundaries effectively, and constructively redirect conversations. This chapter explores how to apply concretization techniques within the Aikido framework to outplay narcissists during conflicts.

Concretization is about transforming vague ideas or feelings into specific, actionable statements. This technique not only enhances understanding but also helps strip away the emotional weight that manipulators often exploit. When faced with manipulation, concretization can help you focus on specifics rather than generalities to regain control of the conversation.

When faced with vague statements, one of the most effective strategies is to ask for clarification. You might respond, "What specific actions do you suggest we take to avoid losing this opportunity?" This question not only puts the onus on the manipulator to provide detailed information but also shifts the focus away from his/her emotional tactics.

In a world where ambiguity can be weaponized, the ability to concretize ideas and demands becomes invaluable. This technique can enhance your communication skills, build stronger relationships, and navigate interpersonal dynamics with confidence and clarity.

9.1 CONCRETIZATION TECHNIQUES IN AIKIDO APPROACHES

Clarifying Your Intentions

Clearly articulate your intentions and goals in the conversation. This technique helps set the stage for constructive dialogue and reduces the chances of misunderstandings.

Application: Instead of saying, "I want us to work better together," you might say, "I would like us to establish weekly check-ins to discuss our progress and address any concerns. This way, we can ensure we're on the same page." By specifying your intention, you create a clear path forward.

Setting Specific Boundaries

Define concrete boundaries of acceptable and unacceptable behavior to establish clear guidelines for interaction and protect your emotional well-being.

Application: If a narcissistic colleague frequently interrupts you during meetings, you could say, "I need to express my ideas fully without interruptions. If you have feedback, I'd appreciate it if you could wait until I finish speaking." This reassertion sets a specific boundary that is easy to understand and enforce.

Providing Concrete Examples

Use specific examples to illustrate your points and clarify your perspectives. This technique helps ground abstract concepts in reality, making it more difficult for a narcissist to dismiss or twist your words.

Application: If a narcissistic partner downplays your contributions, you might say, "Last week, I led the presentation on our project, and I worked late to ensure the report met our deadlines. It's important for me to feel recognized for my efforts." By highlighting specific instances, you reinforce your position with tangible evidence.

Articulating Specific Needs

Express your needs and expectations straightforwardly. This technique helps prevent a narcissist from deflecting the conversation or shifting the focus back to him/herself.

Application: Instead of saying, "I need more support," you could say, "I need you to check in with me at least once a day to discuss our workload and ensure we're aligned. This statement will help me feel supported in our collaboration." This directness makes your needs clear and actionable.

Creating Actionable Plans

Develop specific, actionable plans to address issues or conflicts to not only provide a framework for resolution but also hold both parties accountable for following through.

Application: If there's tension about shared responsibilities at home, you could propose, "Let's create a household chore schedule together. I suggest we outline specific tasks and assign them for the week. We can review it every Sunday to make adjustments." This proposition creates a structured approach to problem-solving.

Utilizing "I" Statements

Frame your feelings and experiences using "I" statements to express your perspective without sounding accusatory. This technique encourages the narcissist to listen rather than become defensive.

Application: Instead of saying, "You never listen to me," you might say, "I feel unheard when I'm interrupted during conversations. I need to share my thoughts fully." This approach focuses on your experience and reduces the likelihood of triggering defensiveness.

Summarizing and Confirming Understanding

After discussing an issue, summarize what has been said to confirm understanding and agreement. This technique ensures clarity and reinforces accountability.

Application: At the end of a discussion, you could say, "To summarize, we've agreed that I will handle the client reports, and you will manage the presentations. Let's check in next week to see how that's working." This proposition ensures that both parties are on the same page and clarifies expectations.

9.2 CASE STUDY #1 - CONCRETIZATION AT WORK

You are in a strategic meeting where your manager states, "If we don't pivot our marketing strategy immediately, we risk losing our top clients!" This statement is laden with emotional urgency and lacks specificity.

Case Study #1:

Manager's manipulative statement:

"If we don't act now, we'll lose our clients!"

Team member's concretized response:

"I appreciate your concern for our client relationships. Can we analyze the key metrics that indicate client satisfaction and retention? Let's **outline** what specific changes we would need to implement and how we can measure their effectiveness."

In this example, you've transformed an emotional appeal into a data-driven discussion, shifting the focus from fear to strategic planning. By doing so, you empower yourself and your team to make informed decisions rather than succumbing to emotional pressure.

Concretization serves as a powerful shield against manipulation, enabling individuals to reclaim control over their conversations and decision-making processes. You can effectively counter vague emotional appeals and foster a more productive environment with clarity, specificity, and collaboration.

9.3 CASE STUDY #2 - CONCRETIZATION IN LOVE RELATIONSHIPS

Your partner frequently expresses frustration about your lack of attention, suggesting that you don't care about the relationship. They might say something like, "You never pay attention to me anymore! If you keep this up, I don't know how we can stay together."

Case Study #2

Your partner's manipulative statement:

"You never pay attention to me anymore! If you keep this up, I don't know how we can stay together."

This statement is emotionally charged and uses absolutes (e.g., "never") that create feelings of guilt and urgency. It puts pressure on you to respond defensively or comply without fully understanding the underlying issues.

Your concretized response:

To counter this manipulation, you can use concretization by clarifying your partner's feelings and specifying what they mean by "attention." Here's how you might respond:

"I hear that you're feeling neglected, and I want to understand this better. Can you give me specific examples of when you've felt I wasn't paying attention? Also, what does 'attention' look like for you? Let's talk about how we can improve this together."

Breakdown of the Concretized Response:

- You start by **acknowledging** your partner's feelings, which shows you care and are willing to listen.
- By asking for specific instances, you encourage your partner to move away from vague assertions and focus on **concrete situations** to help clarify the issue and reduce emotional exaggeration.
- You ask your partner to **define what "attention" means** to him/her to open up a productive dialogue about their needs and expectations, allowing you both to understand each other better.
- By suggesting that you talk about how to improve the situation together, you **shift** the conversation from blame and manipulation to collaboration and problem-solving.

The Outcome

Your concretized response not only diffuses the emotional tension but also opens the door for a constructive conversation. It allows both partners to express their needs and work together to find solutions rather than get caught in a cycle of guilt and defensiveness.

In human relationships, manipulation can often stem from misunderstandings and emotional triggers.

Outplaying a narcissist in conflict requires a balance of assertiveness and adaptability. By employing concretization techniques within the Aikido framework, you can create a more structured and constructive dialogue that minimizes the potential for manipulation or escalation. This approach not only helps you communicate your needs and boundaries effectively but also fosters an environment where both parties can engage in meaningful dialogue.

Remember that while you cannot change a narcissist's behavior, you can control how you respond and navigate the interaction. By being clear and specific, you empower yourself to maintain your integrity and emotional well-being, ultimately leading to healthier relationships and more productive outcomes.

CHAPTER 10
GENERALIZATION AS A COUNTER MANIPULATION TACTIC

In the complex tapestry of human relationships, manipulation often lurks in the shadows. Recognizing manipulation is the first step in countering it. Manipulators often rely on emotional triggers, exaggerations, and ultimatums to steer conversations in their favor. One powerful technique that can serve as a counter-manipulation strategy is generalization. This method involves stepping back from the immediate emotional context of a conversation to recognize broader patterns and themes, ultimately allowing individuals to regain control and foster constructive dialogue. By drawing broader conclusions from specific instances or recognizing patterns of behavior you can form your responses. Awareness enables you to identify recurring themes in the narcissist's behavior, allowing you to anticipate their reactions and adapt your strategies accordingly. By taking a step back, you can diffuse emotionally charged situations and redirect the conversation toward a more productive and rational discussion.

The Aikido approach to conflict resolution emphasizes harmony, fluidity, and non-resistance, enabling individuals to navigate diffi-cult situations without escalating tensions. Generalization techniques can enhance this approach by allowing you to adopt broader, more flexible perspectives in your interactions with narcissistic individuals. This chapter explores how generalization techniques can be integrated into an Aikido framework to effectively manage and potentially outplay a narcissist during conflicts.

One of the key benefits of generalization is that it allows you to view a situation from a broader perspective and understand recurring themes rather than getting bogged down in specific grievances.

Besides, generalization allows for a degree of emotional detachment, which can prevent impulsive reactions driven by guilt or anger.

By identifying patterns, individuals can address systemic issues without getting caught in a cycle of blame and defensiveness.

10.1 TECHNIQUES FOR EFFECTIVE GENERALIZATION

Recognize Patterns

The first step of generalization is to identify recurring themes in your interactions. Recognize and generalize the narcissist's typical responses and behaviors in various situations. By identifying these patterns, you can anticipate their moves and adapt your approach.

Application: If you notice that a narcissistic colleague often seeks to undermine others during team meetings, you can prepare responses in advance. For example, when this colleague dismisses your ideas, you could respond with a structured, evidence-based presentation. By framing your ideas more robustly, you can counter his/her tendency to belittle without engaging in confrontation.

Use Inclusive Language

When responding to manipulation, frame your responses in a way that encourages collaboration. For example, instead of saying, "You always criticize me," you might say, "I've noticed that we often discuss household responsibilities in a way that feels negative. Can we shift the conversation to a more positive approach?"

Focus on Shared Goals

Redirect the conversation toward shared objectives. For instance, if your partner expresses frustration about a specific behavior, respond with, "I understand that the dishes are important to you. Let's talk about how we can both contribute to keeping the house tidy." Generalize shared interests and goals to create a sense of collaboration. By focusing on mutual objectives, you can redirect the conversation away from conflict.

Application: In a negotiation with a narcissistic manager, you might say, "We both want this project to succeed and meet our deadlines. Let's focus on how we can achieve that together." This approach shifts the focus from individual egos to shared success, minimizing the potential for conflict.

Highlight Progress

When discussing issues, emphasize the progress you've made together rather than dwelling on past mistakes. For example, "I know we've had disagreements about chores, but I appreciate how we've both worked to create a more organized home."

Encourage Reflection

Invite the other person to reflect on the broader implications of his/her statements. For instance, "When you say I never help around the house, how does that affect our overall communication? Can we find a way to express our needs without making it personal?"

Use Analogies and Metaphors

Employ analogies or metaphors to illustrate your points and foster understanding. This technique can help you communicate complex ideas in a relatable way, making it harder for a narcissist to dismiss your perspective.

Application: If a narcissistic partner is resistant to your feedback, you might say, "Think of our relationship like a garden. If one plant overgrows the others, the whole garden suffers. We both need to nurture our space for it to flourish." This generalization helps your partner understand the importance of balance and collaboration without feeling personally attacked.

Framing Situations in Broader Terms

Frame the conflict in broader, universal terms that appeal to common values or principles. This technique helps depersonalize the conflict and encourage a more constructive dialogue.

Application: If a narcissistic friend frequently puts his/her needs above yours, you might say, "In any healthy relationship, both individuals should feel valued and respected. Let's ensure we're both contributing equally to our friendship." This framing encourages them to reflect on their behavior in the context of broader relational dynamics.

Highlighting Long-Term Consequences

Generalize the potential long-term effects of their behavior on relationships and outcomes to help narcissists see the broader implications of their actions besides their immediate desires.

Application: If a narcissistic coworker is focusing solely on his/her success, you might say, "When we prioritize teamwork and support each other, we not only achieve our goals but also build a stronger reputation and relationships within the company." This perspective encourages him/her to consider the benefits of collaboration over individualism.

Creating a Narrative Shift

Generalize your experiences and the experiences of others to create a narrative that highlights positive outcomes of collaboration and respect.

Application: If a narcissistic family member insists on his/her viewpoint, you could say, "I've seen how relationships thrive when everyone feels heard and respected. Let's try to find a solution that acknowledges both our perspectives." This shift in narrative encourages a more inclusive approach to the conflict.

Using Non-Verbal Cues

Generalize positive body language and tone of voice to create a calm and inviting atmosphere. This technique can help de-escalate tensions and foster a more constructive dialogue.

Application: During a contentious discussion with a narcissist, maintain open body language, make eye contact, and use a calm tone. You might say, "I appreciate your passion for this topic. Let's explore how we can both express our ideas without stepping on each other's toes." Your demeanor can influence the narcissist's response and encourage a more collaborative interaction.

Integrating generalization techniques into an Aikido approach can significantly enhance your ability to navigate conflicts with narcissistic individuals. By recognizing patterns, establishing common ground, using analogies, framing discussions in broader terms, highlighting long-term consequences, creating narrative shifts, and utilizing positive non-verbal cues, you can effectively manage interactions without escalating tensions or compromising your values.

The key to successfully applying these techniques lies in maintaining a mindset of empathy and understanding, even in challenging situations. By focusing on the larger picture and recognizing the shared humanity in others—even those with narcissistic tendencies—you can foster a more constructive dialogue and encourage healthier interactions.

10.2 PRACTICAL APPLICATION: STEPS TO IMPLEMENT

To effectively apply these generalization techniques in your conflicts with narcissists, consider the following steps:

Observe and Reflect

- Pay close attention to the narcissist's behavior patterns over time.
- Reflect on past interactions to identify recurring themes that can inform your future responses.

Prepare Your Responses

- Anticipate potential arguments or actions from the narcissist and develop generalized responses that address his/her behavior without confrontation.
- Practice framing your ideas in terms of shared goals and values.

Use Analogies

- Think of relatable analogies or metaphors that can convey your message effectively.
- Prepare a few examples in advance that resonate with the context of your relationship.

Maintain a Broader Perspective

- Whenever conflict arises, remind yourself of the larger context and the importance of collaboration over individualism.

- Consider how the situation fits into a broader narrative of mutual respect and cooperation.

Foster Open Communication

- Use positive body language and an open tone to create a welcoming environment for dialogue.
- Encourage the narcissist to express his/her perspective while also asserting your own needs and boundaries.

Document Patterns

- Keep a record of specific instances of narcissistic behavior and your responses. This can help you recognize patterns and refine your strategies over time.

CASE STUDY

During a heated discussion, your partner says, "You never listen to me! You're always too busy with your phone to care about what I'm saying!"

Your partner's manipulative statement: "You never listen to me! You're always too busy with your phone!"

Your generalized response: Instead of reacting defensively, you could respond, "I can see that you feel unheard, and that's important to address. I've noticed that we both sometimes get caught up in our phones during conversations. Let's find a way to create clearer boundaries for our time together so we can focus on each other better."

Breakdown of the Generalized Response:

Acknowledge feelings: You validate your partner's feelings, showing empathy and understanding.

Identify a pattern: By recognizing a broader issue (both of you being distracted by phones), you step away from the individual accusation.

Propose a solution: Instead of becoming defensive, you suggest working together to create a solution, fostering collaboration and communication.

The Outcome

This generalized response not only diffuses the emotional intensity of the original statement but also transforms the conversation into a constructive dialogue about shared behaviors and goals. It allows both partners to express their feelings while focusing on solutions rather than blame.

In romantic relationships, generalization serves as a powerful counter-manipulation technique. By taking a step back to identify patterns and broader themes, individuals can transform their attitude, react with calm, and avoid escalation of a conflict.

Outplaying a narcissist in conflict does not mean defeating him/her in a traditional sense; rather, it involves skillfully navigating the interaction to maintain your integrity and emotional well-being. By applying generalization techniques within the Aikido framework, you can effectively manage conflicts, assert your boundaries, and foster healthier dynamics.

CHAPTER 11
SCRIPT BREAKING

This chapter describes the concept of script breakdown as a counter-manipulation strategy, providing you with practical tools and insights to reclaim your power in relationships.

Breaking a narcissist's script in conflict resolution requires strategic communication techniques and a strong understanding of narcissistic behavior. Narcissists often rely on certain predictable patterns, i.e. scripts, they use to manipulate, deflect, or dominate conversations. By disrupting these scripts, you can regain control of the dialogue and foster more constructive outcomes. Here are several strategies to help you break these scripts effectively.

Understanding the common scripts narcissists use is the first step toward breaking them. These may include:

- Victimhood: They may portray themselves as the victim to elicit sympathy or deflect blame.
- Gaslighting: They may deny your reality or make you question your perceptions.

- Blame Shifting: They often redirect blame onto you or others instead of taking responsibility.
- Triangulation: They may involve a third party to validate their perspective or create conflict.

Narcissists thrive on emotional reactions. By staying calm and composed, you can prevent them from gaining power over you.

The first thing to remember - **pause** before responding. Take a moment to gather your thoughts before responding to emotionally charged statements. You can practice deep breathing techniques to maintain your composure and reduce anxiety.

Clarity is essential in breaking a narcissist's script. Avoid ambiguity in your statements. Instead of saying, "I'd like us to communicate better," say, "I want to set aside 15 minutes every day to discuss our work progress."

Instead of asking, "What do you think?" use closed questions that require a specific response, such as, "Can you agree to meet at 3 PM tomorrow?"

When narcissists attempt to manipulate the conversation, you can **reframe** their statements to redirect the focus. The next chapter covers in more detail the reframing techniques. Here, I will limit myself to two simple examples to demonstrate how reframing can redirect the conversation.

If a manipulator plays the victim, acknowledge his/her feelings but redirect the conversation. For example, "I understand you feel overwhelmed, but we need to focus on how we can solve this issue together."

If they shift blame onto you, respond with, "I hear your concerns, but let's discuss how we can both take responsibility for our roles in this situation."

Establishing clear **boundaries** is crucial in preventing narcissistic manipulation by using "I" Statements**. Frame boundaries in terms of your needs. For example, "I need to be treated with respect during our conversations. Interrupting me makes it difficult for us to resolve our issues." Be consistent. Consistently enforce your boundaries. If they attempt to cross them, remind them of the boundary you've set.

Narcissists seek emotional reactions to manipulate situations. Therefore, **limit your emotional engagement**.

Stay Neutral. Respond to provocations with neutrality. Instead of reacting emotionally, say, "I see this is important to you, but I'd like to keep our discussion focused on finding a solution."

Keep the conversation focused on behaviors and issues rather than personal attributes. For example, say, "The way we handled the last project wasn't effective," instead of, "You always mess things up."

Silence can be a powerful tool in breaking a narcissist's script.

After a manipulative statement, use silence to create discomfort. Pause strategically to prompt the narcissists to rethink their approach.

Let Them Fill the Void. A narcissist may feel compelled to fill the silence, which can lead him/her to reveal more about their motivations.

Keeping a record can help you maintain clarity in conflicts. Keep notes of significant discussions that you can refer back to if needed to help counteract gaslighting. Share your perspective with trusted friends or colleagues to validate your experiences externally.

If conflicts become overwhelming, consider involving a neutral third party.

Last, but not the least, know when to walk away. Sometimes, the most effective way to break a narcissist's script is to disengage completely.

If the conversation becomes unproductive or abusive, it's okay to excuse yourself. You can say, "I think it's best if we take a break and revisit this conversation later when we're both calmer." This approach preserves your well-being and puts the onus on the narcissist to reflect on their behavior.

Breaking narcissists' scripts in conflict resolution requires a blend of assertiveness, clarity, and emotional intelligence. Using the strategies outlined above will allow you to disrupt their manipulative patterns and foster more constructive dialogue.

In addition to these strategies, it's essential to build your resilience when dealing with narcissists. Understanding narcissistic behavior can empower you to navigate interactions more effectively. Read books, attend workshops, or join support groups focused on dealing with narcissism.

Managing conflicts with narcissists is undoubtedly challenging, but the strategies outlined above can help you create a more balanced dynamic. Remember that while you cannot change narcissists' behaviors, you can control your responses and assert your needs. By breaking their scripts and fostering clear communication, you can navigate conflicts more effectively and protect your emotional well-being.

Ultimately, the goal is to create healthier interactions, whether that means finding common ground, establishing boundaries, or knowing when to disengage for your peace of mind. Stay strong, and remember that you deserve to be treated with respect and dignity in all your relationships. You have the power to shape your relationships and experiences. By approaching interactions with awareness and assertiveness, you can create a life that aligns with your values and aspirations.

CHAPTER 12

EMPOWERMENT THROUGH KNOWLEDGE AND ACTION

The power of understanding and grasping the nuanced threads that compose the fabric of narcissistic behavior cannot be overstated. It is akin to turning on a light in a room that has been shrouded in darkness, revealing both the obstacles and the exits with clarity. This chapter is dedicated to fortifying you with this luminous knowledge, offering tools and strategies that not only enhance your understanding but also help you act with informed confidence.

12.1 EDUCATIONAL EMPOWERMENT: CONTINUOUS LEARNING ABOUT NARCISSISM

In the realm of dealing with narcissists, ignorance is far from bliss. Knowledge, continuously updated and refreshed, serves as your armor and guide. It is vital to stay abreast of the latest research on narcissism as the field of psychology continually evolves to understand and develop new coping strategies. Recent studies and expert analyses can transform your approach and response to narcissistic behavior from reactive to proactive, from uncertain to precise.

A commitment to education is a cornerstone of empowerment. As such, I recommend a curated list of essential readings that serve as a foundation for understanding the complex nature of narcissism and the journey to recovery. Books such as *The Wizard of Oz and Other Narcissists* by Eleanor Payson offer insights into recognizing and dealing with narcissistic personalities in various relationships. Articles in psychology journals and periodicals like *Psychology Today* frequently discuss the latest research findings and therapeutic approaches, providing up-to-date information that can help refine your strategies for handling narcissistic interactions. Additionally, memoirs and personal stories of those who have navigated relationships with narcissists can offer both solace and practical advice.

Participation in workshops and seminars that focus on narcissism and related psychological topics is another powerful method for deepening your understanding. These meetings provide opportunities not only to learn from experts but also to connect with others who are in similar situations. For instance, seminars led by renowned psychologists or therapists specializing in narcissistic abuse can elucidate aspects of narcissist behavior that may be obscure or confusing and provide new coping techniques in a supportive group setting.

Moreover, the digital age offers unprecedented access to knowledge through online courses. Engaging with these resources not only enhances your understanding but also empowers you to make informed decisions about how to manage your interactions with narcissists effectively.

Through continuous learning, you build a robust framework of understanding that transforms your interactions with narcissists. This ongoing educational journey ensures that you are always equipped with the latest strategies and knowledge, enabling you to handle narcissistic behaviors with confidence and efficacy.

12.2 CREATING AN ACTION PLAN: STEPS FOR LONG-TERM FREEDOM

In navigating the complexities of relationships with narcissists, crafting a well-defined action plan is akin to drawing a detailed map for a journey through uncharted territory. It provides direction, sets expectations, and prepares you for potential challenges along the way. The first step in this process is to define clear, achievable objectives for your recovery and interactions with narcissists. Whether it's establishing firm boundaries, reducing contact, or fully disengaging from the narcissist, each goal should reflect your personal needs and circumstances. For example, if continuous interaction with a narcissistic family member is unavoidable, you might focus on maintaining emotional detachment during interactions to preserve your mental health. Alternatively, if you're planning to exit a narcissistic relationship, your goal could be to strengthen your emotional and financial independence.

Once your objectives are set, the next step involves detailed, step-by-step planning, which involves breaking down your main objectives into smaller, manageable goals, each with specific, actionable steps. Suppose one of your objectives is to reduce emotional distress caused by a narcissistic partner. In that case, short-term goals might include scheduling regular therapy sessions, practicing daily mindfulness exercises to enhance emotional regulation, or establishing a support network of friends who understand your situation. Each of these goals requires specific actions, such as researching therapists who specialize in narcissistic abuse, setting aside time each day for meditation, or joining a local support group. This breakdown not only makes the tasks more digestible but also provides clear milestones to track your progress.

The importance of regular review and adjustment in your action plan cannot be overstated. As situations evolve and new insights are gained, your strategies may need to be refined or redirected. This adaptive approach ensures that your plan remains relevant and effectively meets your needs. Regular check-ins, perhaps bi-weekly or monthly, provide opportunities to assess what's working and what isn't. During these reviews, you might find that certain strategies are not as effective as anticipated or that new challenges require adjustments to your approach. For example, if you find that your stress levels are not decreasing despite regular meditation, you might decide to try alternative relaxation techniques, such as yoga or tai chi.

Finally, documenting your action plan plays a crucial role in reinforcing your commitment to your goals and tracking your progress. Keeping a journal or digital document where you record your strategies, adjustments, and reflections acts as both a roadmap and a logbook. It allows you to see how far you've come, which can be incredibly affirming and motivating. Documenting your journey also helps maintain clarity of purpose, ensuring that each step you take is aligned with your overall objectives. This record can be particularly valuable during moments of doubt or when the manipulative tactics of the narcissist might otherwise cloud your judgment.

By following these steps - defining clear objectives, planning meticulously, regularly reviewing and adjusting your strategy, and documenting your progress - you create a dynamic and effective action plan that guides you toward long-term freedom and recovery from narcissistic abuse. This structured approach not only empowers you to navigate the challenges posed by the narcissist but also supports your overall growth and healing, paving the way for a future where your well-being and peace of mind take precedence.

12.3 ROLE-PLAYING SCENARIOS: PRACTICING YOUR RESPONSES

Imagine finding yourself in a familiar yet uncomfortable situation with a narcissist - perhaps a conversation that starts benignly but predictably spirals into manipulation or criticism. Here, role-playing emerges as a powerful tool, a rehearsal for real life that empowers you to navigate and counter manipulative tactics effectively. Developing custom scenarios based on your specific experiences with narcissists allows you to anticipate likely challenges and practice your responses. For instance, if you often find yourself undermined in personal discussions, you could create a scenario where you practice asserting your perspective confidently despite interruptions or belittlement.

The process of constructing these scenarios involves detailed scripting of potential dialogues, considering both verbatim manipulations you've encountered and your ideal responses. This practice enables you to transition from reactive to proactive interactions. It involves changing the scripts from past encounters when you might have felt disempowered into new ones that reinforce your autonomy and respect. To enhance realism, incorporate typical verbal and non-verbal cues that the narcissist might display, such as dismissive gestures or condescending tones, which will help you practice maintaining composure under pressure.

Guidance on conducting these role-playing exercises effectively often begins with creating a safe, controlled environment where you can express emotions without judgment. This setup is crucial as it allows you to fully engage with the scenario without real-world repercussions. Begin each session with a clear outline of the scenario, and as you progress, allow for some flexibility in responses to simulate the unpredictability of real interactions. Feedback during these sessions is invaluable. It provides insights into how your responses might be perceived and allows you to refine them to ensure they are both assertive and respectful.

Involving trusted friends or family members in these exercises can enhance their effectiveness. These individuals can offer perspectives on your responses, suggest alternative strategies, or even play the role of the narcissist, providing a dynamic that closely mirrors real interactions. Their feedback can help you identify when your responses might be too passive or unnecessarily confrontational, allowing you to adjust your approach accordingly. Moreover, their support can reinforce your emotional resilience, reminding you that you are not alone in these experiences.

For those seeking more structured guidance, professional role-playing sessions with therapists or coaches who specialize in narcissistic abuse can be exceptionally beneficial. These professionals can offer a more nuanced understanding of narcissistic behaviors and provide expert feedback on your handling of the scenarios. They can also introduce more complex interaction simulations to challenge you to apply your emotional intelligence and assertiveness in various contexts. This professional input ensures that your responses not only address the immediate manipulations but also contribute to a long-term strategy of empowerment and self-respect.

Engaging in these role-playing scenarios equips you with not just the strategies but also the confidence to handle interactions with narcissists more effectively. By rehearsing your responses, you transform theoretical knowledge into practical skills, ready to be deployed in real-world situations. This preparation can make all the difference, turning potential confrontations into opportunities for asserting your boundaries and reclaiming your power in relationships marred by manipulation.

12.4 BUILDING A SUPPORTIVE NETWORK: IDENTIFYING ALLIES

In the often isolating experience of dealing with narcissistic abuse, discovering and nurturing relationships with allies can be as revitalizing as a rain shower on a parched garden. These allies are individuals within your personal, professional, and social circles who not only understand the complexities of narcissistic abuse but also provide the support, empathy, and validation needed to navigate this challenging path. Identifying potential allies begins with keen observation and interaction; therefore, pay close attention to how people react when topics related to emotional manipulation or personal difficulties are discussed. Those who respond with empathy, offer supportive insights, or share their own experiences with understanding are likely candidates. It's also beneficial to look for individuals who consistently demonstrate emotional intelligence, as they're more likely to grasp the subtle dynamics involved in abusive relationships and offer meaningful support.

Once potential allies are identified, the next crucial step is to cultivate these relationships beyond casual interactions, which requires intentional efforts to deepen connections. Regular communication that involves sharing experiences, thoughts, and feelings is key when dealing not only with narcissistic abuse but also with other aspects of life, as it helps build trust and mutual understanding. Engaging in activities together, whether attending support groups, participating in social events, or simply having coffee, can strengthen these bonds. It's important to ensure these relationships are reciprocal; just as you benefit from others' support, be sure to offer your support and understanding in their times of need. This reciprocity fosters a deeper connection and mutual respect, forming a solid foundation for a supportive relationship.

Online support groups offer another valuable resource for building your network of allies. These platforms allow you to connect with individuals from around the globe who are navigating similar challenges. Many online forums and social media groups are dedicated to discussions about narcissistic abuse—providing a space to share stories, strategies, and encouragement. Participating in these groups can significantly broaden your support network, giving you access to a wealth of collective knowledge and experiences. When selecting an online group, look for one that maintains a positive and constructive tone, actively moderates discussions to prevent negativity or trolling, and respects the privacy and confidentiality of its members. Engaging with these communities not only helps you feel less alone but also equips you with diverse strategies for dealing with narcissists, enhancing your ability to manage your situation effectively.

The role of allies in your recovery from narcissistic abuse cannot be overstated. They provide a sounding board for your thoughts and feelings, offer practical advice that can help you navigate the legal and emotional complexities of your situation, and validate your experiences and feelings. This support is crucial in reaffirming your reality, especially when it has been distorted by a narcissist's manipulations. Allies can also play a significant role in helping you regain confidence and rebuild your sense of self-worth. Their belief in your strengths and their encouragement as you make tough decisions or take steps toward recovery can be incredibly empowering. Moreover, a network of supportive allies serves as a protective buffer against the narcissist's attempts to isolate you, enhancing your resilience and ability to stand firm in your boundaries.

In cultivating this network, it's essential to maintain openness to new relationships while nurturing existing ones, continuously expanding and strengthening your circle of support. As you do so, you not only enhance your recovery and resilience but also contribute to a broader community of support and understanding, which can be invaluable to others with similar experiences. This reciprocal exchange of support and understanding enriches your journey and contributes to a culture of empathy and resilience, making it a vital aspect of healing and growth.

12.5 USING TECHNOLOGY: APPS AND TOOLS FOR MENTAL HEALTH

In an era where technology intersects with almost every aspect of our lives, it has also become a pivotal ally in managing mental health, particularly when navigating the complexities of narcissistic abuse. Apps specifically designed to support mental health can offer accessible, immediate resources that help manage stress, track emotional trends, and provide strategies for relaxation and coping. For instance, meditation apps like Headspace and Calm provide guided sessions that can help center your thoughts and calm your mind, which is especially beneficial after stressful interactions with a narcissist. These apps often include sessions specifically designed to deal with anxiety or stress, making them a valuable tool in your emotional toolkit.

Additionally, mood tracker apps - Mood Tracker, Mind and other - enable you to record your daily emotional experiences, helping you identify patterns or triggers in your interactions with narcissists. These insights can be crucial in understanding how certain behaviors affect your emotional well-being and can guide you in making informed decisions about how to manage these interactions. For example, you might notice that discussions about certain topics consistently lead to a decline in your mood, prompting you to either avoid these topics or prepare more thoroughly before engaging in them. This kind of self-awareness is critical in maintaining emotional equilibrium and ensuring that you are not unconsciously pulled into the narcissist's emotional manipulations.

Safety and privacy apps also play a crucial role, especially for those who may need to block communication from a narcissist or ensure their digital interactions remain private. Apps that offer end-to-end encryption for messages and calls - Signal, Telegram, Briar and other - ensure that your communication is secure from prying eyes, which can be a concern if a narcissist tries to invade your privacy or monitor your interactions. Furthermore, apps designed to block calls or messages from specific numbers can provide peace of mind, as they can prevent a narcissist from contacting you, which can be especially important during periods of no contact or after leaving an abusive relationship. These tools not only enhance your safety but also reinforce your boundaries, making it clear that harassment or unwanted contact will not be tolerated.

Educational apps that focus on narcissism and psychological health can provide valuable information to help you understand and deal with narcissistic behaviors more effectively. They offer articles, quizzes, and interactive content on topics related to mental health, including detailed sections on personality disorders and coping mechanisms. These resources make complex psychological concepts accessible and provide practical advice that you can apply in your interactions with narcissists. By integrating these educational apps into your daily routine, you can continuously expand your knowledge and skills, which is essential for those who find themselves frequently dealing with narcissistic individuals.

These apps should be incorporated into your daily life, which requires consistent rather than only occasional engagement with the tools and resources they provide. Set reminders to meditate daily with your chosen app, or schedule regular times to update your mood tracker. This consistent usage maximizes the benefits of these apps, making them integral parts of your strategy to manage mental health and deal with narcissistic abuse. Regular use ensures that the insights, coping strategies, and educational content provided by these apps are continuously incorporated into your life, strengthening your resilience and empowering you to maintain your mental health in the face of challenges.

By leveraging these technological tools, you equip yourself with immediate, accessible support that enhances your ability to manage stress, understand and block harmful interactions, and educate yourself about narcissism. The integration of technology into your mental health strategy not only supports your recovery and coping mechanisms but also empowers you to live a more balanced, informed, and secure life.

12.6 CELEBRATING SMALL VICTORIES: TRACKING PROGRESS

In the intricate dance with narcissism, each step forward, no matter how small, is a testament to your resilience and a building block towards a stronger self. Recognizing and celebrating these small victories is crucial, as they collectively form the path out of the shadow of manipulation. Setting measurable milestones is the first step in this celebration. These milestones, such as successfully maintaining boundaries in a conversation with a narcissist or managing to remain calm during a typically triggering interaction, act as markers of your progress. For instance, you might set a goal to not respond immediately to provocative texts from a narcissist, giving yourself time to formulate a calm, measured response. Achieving this can significantly boost your confidence and reinforce your ability to handle similar situations in the future.

Keeping a success journal is another powerful tool in this process. This journal serves as a tangible record of your progress, where every entry is a victory. Each time you successfully implement a strategy learned from your interactions or educational pursuits, jot it down. Writing about these successes reinforces the positive outcomes of your efforts and can be incredibly uplifting, especially on days when progress seems slow or invisible. This journal does not need to be elaborate—a simple notebook or digital document can suffice. The act of writing helps solidify the reality of your achievements, making them more concrete and undeniable.

Sharing these achievements plays a pivotal role in solidifying them. Discussing your progress with a therapist, a support group, or trusted friends not only provides an external validation but also encourages continued growth. These discussions can be profoundly affirming, particularly when you are met with understanding and encouragement. They remind you that you are not alone on this path and that others support and recognize your efforts. Moreover, sharing your journey can inspire and educate others who might be dealing with similar challenges, creating a ripple effect of empowerment and insight within your support network.

Reflective practice is integral to this celebration of victories. Regularly reviewing your success journal allows you to see not just individual achievements but also patterns of growth over time. A monthly or annual review of your entries would let you see how far you've come. During these reviews, you might notice that strategies that were once difficult to implement have become second nature or that your emotional responses to certain triggers have become less intense. These insights are invaluable as they not only highlight your progress but also help identify areas that might require more focus or adjustment. Reflecting on your experiences and achievements ensures that your approach to dealing with narcissism remains dynamic and responsive to your evolving needs and circumstances.

In embracing and celebrating each small victory, you affirm your journey towards a life defined not by the presence of a narcissist but by your strength and resilience. These celebrations keep you anchored in the positive aspects of your growth, fueling your journey forward with hope and confidence. They remind you that every effort, no matter how minor it might seem, is a crucial step towards reclaiming your autonomy and crafting a life full of respect and fulfillment.

As this chapter concludes, we reflect on the powerful role of tracking and celebrating your progress in your overall recovery and empowerment. Each small victory is a step out of the shadows of doubt and manipulation and into the light of self-assurance and independence. As you continue to set milestones, record your successes, share your achievements, and reflect on your growth, you build a solid foundation of self-validation and resilience. Armed with these strategies, you are better equipped to navigate the challenges posed by narcissism and to move forward into the next stages of your journey with confidence and clarity. In the following chapter, we will explore advanced strategies for maintaining and enhancing these gains, ensuring that your progress is not only maintained but accelerated as you continue to build a life defined by strength and self-respect.

CHAPTER 13
STAYING AHEAD: LONG-TERM STRATEGIES AND ART OF ANTICIPATION

In the nuanced theater of human relationships, recognizing the masks people wear is both an art and a survival skill. For those entangled with narcissists, this skill is not just about seeing through disguises but also about maintaining the strength of your character and boundaries over time. As the allure of the narcissist's initial charm fades, the continuous challenge is to reinforce your defenses, ensuring they stand firm against future manipulation attempts. This chapter is dedicated to arming you with strategies that ensure your boundaries are not just established but also maintained and adapted as you navigate the complexities of these relationships over the long haul.

13.1 LONG-TERM BOUNDARY MAINTENANCE: KEEPING DEFENSES STRONG

Reinforcement of Boundaries

Boundaries with a narcissist are not static; they require vigilance and continual reinforcement to remain effective. The importance of regularly reinforcing boundaries cannot be overstated - it's akin to maintaining the walls of a fortress that keeps potential psychological invaders at bay. This reinforcement involves clear communication of your limits and consistent actions that match your words. For example, if you have decided not to engage in conversations about your personal life at work, your ex-partner, or any other experience to avoid a narcissist's manipulative comments, consistently redirecting discussions back to different topics whenever attempts are made to cross this boundary is a practical reinforcement strategy. It's about being firm and consistent, not just once but every time the boundary is tested.

Scheduled Boundary Reviews

Just as businesses conduct periodic reviews to ensure they are on track with their goals, scheduling regular reviews of your boundaries can be incredibly beneficial. These reviews allow you to assess the effectiveness of your boundaries and make necessary adjustments based on new dynamics or challenges. Perhaps a boundary set months ago needs tweaking because the narcissist has found a subtle way around it, or maybe changes in your personal or professional life require a shift in your defensive strategies. Biannual or annual reviews, where you reflect on each boundary's strength and utility, can help you stay two steps ahead of any manipulative tactics that might be brewing.

Support From Others

Maintaining strong boundaries can sometimes feel like a solitary battle, but it doesn't have to be. Seeking feedback and support from trusted friends, family members, or professionals can play a crucial role in strengthening your boundary-setting practices. These individuals can offer an outside perspective on your situation, perhaps pointing out blind spots in your defenses or rein-forcing your commitment to upholding your boundaries. They can also provide emotional support, reminding you that you're not alone in this struggle and that maintaining boundaries is both healthy and necessary for your well-being.

Teach Assertive Reinforcement Techniques

Effective boundary maintenance often requires assertive commu-nication - expressing your needs clearly and respectfully without aggression. Teaching yourself assertive reinforcement techniques can be a game-changer. This approach might include learning to use phrases like, "As I mentioned before, I'm not comfortable discussing this topic. Let's focus on…" or "I understand you have a different view, but I need to stick to my decision on this." For more physical boundaries, techniques might involve controlling your body language, like stepping back or using a hand gesture that signifies 'stop.' Workshops, books, or sessions with a commu-nication coach can provide valuable training in these areas.

In reinforcing your boundaries, you reclaim your power from the narcissist's grip, shaping interactions on your terms. This constant process of reinforcement ensures that your defenses remain robust, adaptable, and reflective of your current emotional and psychological landscape, allowing you to navigate your relationship with confidence and clarity.

13.2 ADVANCED COPING MECHANISMS: DEALING WITH NEW NARCISSISTIC ATTACKS

In navigating relationships with narcissists, staying ahead involves more than recognizing patterns; it demands a proactive stance - anticipating potential behaviors and crafting strategic responses ahead of time. The art of anticipation is not about predicting the future with perfect accuracy but about preparing for probable scenarios based on past interactions. This proactive approach allows you to cultivate a sense of control and readiness, reducing the chances of being caught off-guard by sudden narcissistic maneuvers. For instance, if a narcissist has previously used guilt trips during family gatherings to manipulate you, planning how you will respond to or deflect these tactics can prevent emotional turmoil. You might decide in advance to change the subject or to respond with neutral, non-committal comments that don't feed into the drama, effectively stalling the narcissist's attempts at manipulation.

Developing emotional buffers forms a critical part of this anticipatory strategy. Emotional buffers, such as detachment techniques and mindfulness, help minimize the effects of the narcissist's actions on your emotional state. Detachment here refers to maintaining an emotional distance that allows you to observe and interact with the narcissist without becoming emotionally entangled. It might involve viewing interactions more as a chess game, where you are a strategist rather than an emotionally involved participant. Mindfulness, on the other hand, helps maintain this detachment by keeping you centered and focused in the present moment, reducing the likelihood of reactive emotional responses. Regular mindfulness practices, such as daily meditation or mindful walking, can strengthen your ability to remain calm and composed, even in the face of provocation.

Advanced de-escalation strategies are also vital, especially in preventing conflicts from escalating into emotional battles that drain your energy and destabilize your emotional health. One effective technique is to use validating statements that acknowledge the narcissist's feelings without agreeing with their distorted perceptions. For example, saying, "I can see you're really passionate about this topic," recognizes their emotional state without confirming or supporting their potentially manipulative content. It helps diffuse tension and steer the conversation into less confrontational waters. Another strategy involves setting conversational boundaries, clearly stating that you will remove yourself from the discussion if it becomes disrespectful or overly heated to protect your emotional well-being and set a clear standard for the type of communication you are willing to engage in.

Scenario-based learning can further enhance your readiness and confidence in handling such interactions. By creating hypothetical scenarios based on potential narcissistic attacks, you can practice your coping mechanisms in a controlled environment. For instance, writing a script for a planned conversation where you anticipate manipulative tactics can allow you to refine your responses. You might role-play this scenario with a friend or therapist to test the effectiveness of your approach and tweak it based on feedback. These rehearsals can make a significant difference in your real-world interactions, providing you with a toolkit of responses that feel natural and are effective in maintaining your boundaries and emotional stability.

Navigating the turbulent waters of relationships with narcissists requires more than reactive measures - it demands a proactive, strategic approach that prepares you for potential challenges. By anticipating and planning for narcissistic behaviors, developing emotional buffers through detachment and mindfulness, employing advanced de-escalation strategies, and practicing scenario-based learning, you equip yourself with the skills necessary to manage these interactions effectively. This proactive stance not only enhances your ability to cope with narcissistic attacks but also empowers you to maintain your emotional health and personal integrity in the face of ongoing challenges.

13.3 THE IMPORTANCE OF ROUTINE IN EMOTIONAL STABILITY

In the unpredictable dance with a narcissist, where emotional currents can shift dramatically and without warning, anchoring yourself in a structured daily routine is essential for emotional survival. A predictable routine provides a framework of stability that can be incredibly soothing, especially against the backdrop of a relationship characterized by volatility. Establishing a daily routine creates a sense of normalcy and control. It involves setting up islands of peace that you can count on, day in and day out, which is especially critical when other aspects of your life may feel chaotic and out of control.

Think of your daily routine as a personal treaty that guards your time and emotional energy. It might include setting specific times for waking up and going to bed, designated hours for work, periods for meals, and slots for relaxation or social activities. The predictability of these patterns can help buffer the stress that comes from dealing with a narcissist. For example, starting your day with a morning ritual, like a jog or a quiet cup of coffee, can instill a sense of calm and preparedness, no matter what the day throws at you. Similarly, ending your day with a routine, perhaps reading or meditation, can help decompress and process any of the day's emotional baggage, ensuring it does not carry over into the night or the next day.

Integrating healthy habits into your routine further enhances this stability. Regular physical exercise, for instance, isn't just about keeping the body fit; it's a powerful antidote to stress. Exercise releases endorphins, chemicals in the brain that act as natural painkillers and mood elevators. They improve the ability to sleep, which in turn reduces stress. Moreover, exercise can serve as a meditative practice in motion, helping to clear the mind and return it to a neutral state, away from the noise and manipulation you might be battling. Nutrition also plays a crucial role. A balanced diet nourishes the body and, by extension, the mind. Foods rich in omega-3 fatty acids, for example, are known to enhance brain function and mood, which can help counteract the mental drain that often comes from interactions with a narcissist.

Mindfulness practices add another layer of fortification to your routine. Activities like yoga and meditation are great for practicing mental and emotional resilience, in addition to improving physical flexibility and promoting relaxation. They teach you to observe your thoughts and feelings without attachment, allowing you to detach from the chaotic influences around you. Regular practice can help you develop a calm center untouched by external turmoil from which you can observe and respond to narcissistic behaviors without being swept away by them. This center becomes a place of refuge and strength from which you can navigate any storm with clarity and steadiness.

However, while the structure is beneficial, rigidity is not. Life is inherently unpredictable, and situations change - sometimes at a moment's notice. The ability to maintain flexibility within your routine is just as important as the routine itself. Flexibility allows you to adapt to new circumstances without losing the benefits of the structure you've built. It means knowing when to skip a workout because you need an extra hour of sleep or choosing to indulge in a comfort meal on a particularly tough day. This adaptability prevents the routine from becoming a cage and, instead, serves as a dynamic framework that supports your well-being, no matter how the external conditions around you may shift.

In crafting your routine, consider it a personal canvas, a daily work of art that you create to support and stabilize your emotional world. It's a potent tool in your arsenal against the unpredictability of life with a narcissist, providing not just a shield but a source of strength and renewal. By carefully considering what to incorporate - be it exercise, nutrition, mindfulness, or flexibility - you tailor this tool to meet your unique needs and circumstances, ensuring that each day, you are prepared to face whatever challenges may arise.

13.4 FUTURE-PROOFING YOUR EMOTIONAL HEALTH AGAINST NARCISSISTS

In a world where knowledge equates to power, staying updated with the latest research and insights into narcissism and psychological health is crucial. This continuous learning is not just about accumulating information; it's about evolving with the growing body of knowledge that could redefine your strategies for dealing with narcissists. As new studies shed light on the complexities of narcissistic behaviors and the psychological defenses we can employ, you are better prepared to handle future interactions. Therefore, regularly reading new publications, attending updated training sessions, and participating in discussions on online platforms dedicated to psychological health is important. The goal is to keep your understanding of narcissism current, which in turn keeps your defensive strategies both effective and innovative. For instance, new research might reveal a particular interaction style that defuses narcissistic manipulation more effectively, or it might highlight a previously underestimated aspect of narcissists' behaviors that could change how you approach future encounters.

Building advanced emotional resilience is another cornerstone in safeguarding your mental health against narcissistic influences. Techniques such as cognitive-behavioral approaches can help you dissect and reframe the interactions that might otherwise have a lasting negative effect on your psyche. These methods teach you to identify cognitive distortions - often used by narcissists to manipulate reality - and counteract them with rational, balanced thoughts. Resilience training programs, often available through therapists or community health services, can further enhance your ability to withstand psychological stressors, equipping you with tools to manage emotions, build self-esteem, and foster a positive outlook despite adversities. These programs typically involve scenario-based exercises that simulate interactions with narcissists, providing a safe environment to practice new skills and build emotional strength.

Technology also plays a pivotal role in supporting your mental health in the digital age. Various apps and online platforms offer resources for monitoring your emotional health and managing stress and anxiety effectively. These tools range from simple mood trackers that help you identify emotional patterns to more complex systems offering guided meditation, stress management exercises, and connectivity with mental health professionals. By integrating these technological solutions into your daily routine, you have constant support at your fingertips, ready to help you manage your emotional state. For example, after a challenging interaction with a narcissist, you might use a meditation app to regain your calm, or you might access a therapy platform to discuss your feelings with a professional, ensuring that you have the support you need to maintain your emotional equilibrium.

Preventive practices form the last line of defense in future-proofing your emotional health. Engaging in critical thinking and self-reflection exercises helps you analyze past interactions with narcissists and learn from them, reducing the likelihood of falling into similar traps in the future. These practices encourage a deeper understanding of your response patterns and vulnerabilities that narcissists might exploit. By regularly taking time to reflect on these interactions, you develop a clearer understanding of the warning signs and are better prepared to act swiftly and decisively to protect yourself. These exercises also foster a habit of mindfulness, keeping you attuned to the present and engaged in your emotional health, which is essential for recognizing the early signs of manipulative behavior and preventing them from escalating.

Together, these strategies create a comprehensive approach to maintaining your emotional health when dealing with narcissists. From staying informed and building resilience to leveraging technology and engaging in preventive practices, each element plays a crucial role in ensuring you are not just surviving but thriving despite the challenges posed by narcissistic behaviors. As you continue to navigate these complex relationships, remember that your greatest weapon is a well-maintained, resilient, and informed self.

13.5 REFLECTION AND CONTINUOUS GROWTH: LIFELONG PRACTICES

In the ongoing dance with life's challenges, the music never really stops. Particularly when dealing with personalities that thrive on manipulation, the need for inner reflection and growth becomes a continuous rhythm in the melody of your daily life. Embracing the habit of regular self-reflection is akin to tuning your instrument in this ongoing performance, ensuring that every note you play resonates with the authenticity and awareness you've cultivated over time. This practice isn't just about catching flaws or missteps; it's about appreciating the complexity of your evolution and recognizing the areas of growth.

Routine personal journaling serves as a profound tool in this reflective practice. Documenting your experiences, insights, and emotional landscapes allows you to create a living archive of your journey that isn't just a ledger of events; rather, it's a canvas where you paint the vivid emotions, thoughts, and revelations that emerge from your interactions, especially those involving narcissistic dynamics. Over time, this journal grows into a valuable resource for learning and introspection, offering you a mirror of how far you've come and a map showing where you might still want to go. It allows you to trace patterns in your emotional responses and recognize triggers that you've mastered or those that still require attention.

Committing to lifelong learning is another pillar supporting your continuous growth. This commitment goes beyond formal education or professional development; it encompasses a broader, more holistic approach to understanding human behavior, emotional intelligence, and the psychological underpinnings of manipulation. By dedicating yourself to an ongoing exploration of these areas, you equip yourself with an ever-expanding toolkit to handle the complexities of relationships with narcissists. It might involve subscribing to relevant podcasts, attending webinars, or participating in community courses that focus on psychology and personal development. Each step in this learning process not only enhances your ability to deal with narcissists but also enriches your personal life, making you more empathetic, informed, and resilient.

Celebrating milestones in your emotional and psychological growth reinforces the positive changes and hard-earned progress you've made. These celebrations can be simple acknowledgments of moments where you successfully handled a manipulative situation or when you remained calm under pressure that would have otherwise upset you. Each celebration acts as a reinforcement, encouraging the continuation of your growth efforts and solidi-fying the new skills you've developed. Such acknowledgments also serve to remind you that growth is actually happening, providing a motivational boost to continue your efforts.

Through these practices of reflection, journaling, continuous learning, and celebrating milestones, you build a robust defense against the manipulative tactics of narcissists and foster a richer, more insightful self. You transform from someone merely reacting to the world into someone who actively shapes your own experi-ences and responses. This transformation is both liberating and empowering, allowing you to navigate not just the challenges posed by narcissists but any of life's complexities with grace and wisdom.

As this chapter closes, remember that the journey of growth and reflection is not a task with a checkbox but a garden that requires constant tending. Each effort you make in understanding yourself and the world around you plants seeds for a healthier, more resilient future. As you move forward, let these practices light your path and guide you to a life not defined by the shadows of others but illuminated by your insight and strength.

SOCIETAL PERSPECTIVES AND BROADER EFFECTS

As you sit down to watch your favorite TV show or flip through a popular magazine, you might not immediately consider the subtle yet pervasive ways in which media shape our understanding of personality disorders, particularly narcissism. The portrayal of narcissistic behavior across various media platforms not only entertains but also educates, often blurring the lines between dramatic fiction and unsettling reality. In this chapter, we explore the representation of narcissism in media, its effects on public understanding, and the potential of media as an educative tool. Through this analysis, you'll gain deeper insights into the societal perceptions that influence and are influenced by media narratives.

In films, television shows, and news outlets, characters or real-life figures with narcissistic traits often captivate audiences with their charisma and complexity. However, these portrayals can be double-edged swords. On one side, they bring attention to narcissistic personality disorder (NPD), making it a topic of public discussion. On the other side, they often dramatize or oversimplify the condition, leading to misconceptions. For instance, characters depicted in popular TV dramas or films like "Gone Girl" or "House of Cards" exhibit traits of manipulation and a lack of empathy aligned with clinical definitions of narcissism. Yet, these portrayals can exaggerate the malice and strategic intent, embedding a sense of fear and otherness that may not accurately reflect the everyday reality of those who live with or are clinically diagnosed with NPD.

The sensational portrayal of narcissism affects how people perceive and interact with individuals who exhibit similar traits in real life. This media influence can lead to a generalized fear and misunderstanding, where the actions of individuals with NPD are often expected to be cunning and deceitful, overshadowing the complexity of the disorder that often includes a deep-seated sense of insecurity and emotional turmoil. Moreover, these portrayals can skew public perception, making it difficult for those with NPD to seek help or receive empathy from others, as they may be prematurely judged based on media stereotypes.

Despite these challenges, media also holds immense potential as an educational tool. By incorporating expert consultations and real-life experiences in storytelling, media creators can offer more accurate and nuanced representations of narcissism. Educational documentaries and talk shows that feature psychological experts discussing NPD can help demystify the disorder and promote a more informed and compassionate public discourse. For example, docuseries that follow the therapeutic processes of individuals diagnosed with NPD can provide viewers with a deeper understanding of the challenges and strategies to manage the disorder.

Media's presentation of celebrities' confessions of mental health struggles offers a clear example. When a celebrity discloses their diagnosis of NPD, the media's framing of their story can either foster public sympathy or reinforce stigmas. The way these stories are told - whether as tales of personal triumph or as cautionary tales of manipulation - shapes societal attitudes toward all individuals with similar diagnoses. This powerful dynamic underscores the responsibility of media creators to handle such disclosures with sensitivity and depth, avoiding sensationalism in favor of stories that foster understanding and empathy.

Through these discussions, it becomes evident that media does not merely reflect societal views on narcissism but actively shapes them. By critically engaging with media portrayals and advocating for more balanced representations, we can contribute to a more nuanced understanding of narcissism. Such an engagement can, in turn, lead to better support systems and treatment approaches for those affected, reducing the stigma and isolation they often face. As we move forward, let us consider how we, as consumers and critics of media, can influence this narrative, promoting a shift towards representations that are not only informative and empathetic but also deeply transformative.

Narcissistic behavior, while universally recognized in the diagnostic criteria of psychology, manifests differently across cultures, influenced largely by societal norms and values. These cultural variances affect not only the expression of narcissistic traits but also the societal tolerance and recognition of such behaviors. For instance, in cultures that highly value individual achievements and assertiveness, traits associated with narcissism, such as self-promotion and competitiveness, may not only be tolerated but encouraged. Conversely, in societies where communal harmony and humility are prized, these same traits might be viewed as disruptive or disrespectful.

The influence of culture on the expression of narcissistic traits can be seen in the workplace environment across different societies. In a highly individualistic culture, like the United States, for example, assertiveness and a strong personal drive are often deemed essential for career advancement. Behaviors that might be classified as narcissistic in other contexts, such as taking full credit for collaborative work or aggressively outshining colleagues, can sometimes be masked as mere professional assertiveness or a high level of ambition. On the other hand, in more collectivist cultures, such as Japan, the same behaviors could be perceived as selfish and harmony-disrupting, likely to be met with disapproval and social sanction.

The tolerance levels of narcissistic behaviors significantly affect their prevalence and recognition in different societies. In cultures where such traits are seen as advantageous, narcissistic behaviors might not only be prevalent but may go largely unrecognized as problematic because they align with societal values of success and self-reliance. This alignment can complicate both the diagnosis and treatment of narcissistic personality disorder, as pathological behaviors might be indistinguishable from those that are culturally condoned or even rewarded.

Moreover, the role of collectivism versus individualism in fostering or curbing narcissistic tendencies is profound. Individualistic societies, which emphasize personal success and fulfillment, might inadvertently foster narcissistic traits by prioritizing personal over communal well-being. The emphasis on individual achievement and recognition can lead to a heightened focus on the self that aligns with narcissistic tendencies. Collectivist societies, in contrast, which value group harmony and collective goals, might naturally curb manifestations of narcissism. In these cultures, community disapproval of overt self-centered behaviors can serve as a powerful deterrent, promoting more empathetic and group-oriented behaviors.

Cultural approaches to mental health also play a critical role in how narcissistic personality disorder is perceived and treated. In Western cultures, where psychology and psychotherapy are well-established fields, there is generally a greater awareness and acceptance of mental health issues, including personality disorders. This openness encourages individuals to seek help and receive treatment, such as psychotherapy or counseling. In contrast, in many non-Western cultures, mental health issues might still be stigmatized, and psychological disorders could be less likely to be openly discussed or treated. In such environments, behaviors associated with narcissistic personality disorder might be less likely to be recognized as part of a treatable psychological issue and more likely to be dismissed as personal failings or character flaws.

These cultural differences underscore the importance of considering cultural context when assessing, diagnosing, and treating narcissistic behavior. Mental health professionals must be culturally competent and aware of how societal norms and values shape the expression and recognition of narcissistic traits. This awareness is crucial for accurate diagnosis and effective treatment, as well as for a broader understanding of how narcissism is viewed and managed in different cultural settings. As we continue to explore the complexities of narcissism across cultural landscapes, it becomes clear that the interplay between individual behavior and societal values is intricate and deeply influential, shaping both the lives of individuals and the fabric of the societies they inhabit.

As the awareness continues to grow, the hope is that narcissistic abuse will be universally recognized and robustly challenged, with comprehensive support systems in place to aid those affected. Education plays a pivotal role in shaping our understanding of the world and ourselves, influencing how we navigate complex social landscapes, including our interpersonal relationships.

Raising awareness of narcissism is a proactive measure. By informing individuals about the characteristics of narcissistic behaviors and their effects on relationships, we can empower people to make informed decisions about their interpersonal engagements. It involves promoting self-awareness and emotional intelligence in addition to identifying the traits of narcissism to help individuals understand their boundaries and methods of counter-manipulation.

ABOUT THE AUTHOR

As a gallerist, author, advocate for women's rights, an active member of the National Association of Women Business Owners (NAWBO), the National Organization for Women (NOW), and the Women's Chamber of Commerce of Palm Beach, Gulbrandsen collaborates with like-minded individuals to drive positive change and create opportunities in business and society.

Gulbrandsen's books serve as a platform to inspire and empower both men and women to break barriers and pursue their dreams fearlessly. Her latest releases, *"Sleeping with a Narcissist"* and *"Checkmate Narcissist"*, focus on the complexities of narcissistic relationships, and their often-overlooked impact on mental health and well-being.

With a deep commitment to helping individuals navigate the challenges posed by narcissism, Gulbrandsen aims to provide readers with a comprehensive understanding of manipulative tactics, offering insights and practical strategies for breaking through, healing, and empowerment.